Table of Cont

THE ONE

Finding Reality
&
The Awakening of
Spiritual Awareness

Keith Loy

Introduction

Throughout a thirty year period, I have lived immersed in an illusion which I mistakenly referred to as 'me'. As I awakened each morning from the night time slumber, I merely slipped without demur from one kind of dream into another. It was this daytime dream which I called 'me'. This dream captivated and hypnotized my awareness with a great fallacy. Like a veil or mask pulled over my eyes, it created an altered 'reality' within my mind, obscuring the Truth of my being. Indeed, this dream totally obliterated the beauty and Oneness of actual Reality from being registered upon my awareness at all.

Yet as it turned out, this illusion I called 'me' was like a castle in the air. It was a thought construct, built from memories of my past. These memories caused a hypnotic spell (what I believed myself to be) to be weaved within my awareness. As this tapestry called 'me' became tightly weaved, I began to mistake the tapestry to be what I am. The tapestry I called 'me' was weaved from thoughts. These thoughts built up a picture in my mind that I could relate to, or a mask I could project upon the world. I spent all of my energy in a vain and useless attempt, to project upon the world what I felt I needed to be, to satisfy the intruding view of others opinions and judgements upon my life.

This has made for such a struggle, this constant maintenance of thought and belief. This has been soul destroying, this continuous projection upon the world of a fictional character made from thoughts of who I wish to be, and who I think I have to be, according to the dictates of society's norms. And all of this effort was so I could have an apparently stable sense of 'self', which I am supposed to 'know' and be able to consistently relate to.

Thought layered upon thought, I built the construct of unreality within my mind. With each thought brick it got intolerably heavier to bear its weight. I felt my energy; my life force dwindle and wither up like a dried out prune. I barely felt alive never mind awake under this burden of built up ego. I dreamed that someday the Real would dawn upon my awareness, bursting forth new life within me and all around me, enlightening my world and enlivening my mind and being.

Yet I rarely stopped long enough in silence, to consider the thoughts which I painted upon my external mask. I never truly questioned the unreality of such thoughts until they got totally out of hand. I mistook these thoughts to be Reality. Yet I was certain that something within me knew the Truth. I didn't fully know what that was at first, but deep within my awareness, I was partially awakened to the knowledge that the thought made 'me' which I paraded to the audience of my world was fragile, flimsy and had no substantiality or ultimate reality at all.

Then one day I wondered - what am I really?

Am I a self of random chance, emerging from a mess of conditioned thought programmes, which the world thinks it knows so well - which I think I know so well? Possibly I am the self which I need to *believe* I am, just so I can fit into this hypnotized world of clone like sameness. Am I similar to one of the pied pipers rats, which unquestioningly and hypnotically follows the tune of the pied piper and his inharmonious melody, dancing to the repetitive beat of societies unrelenting conditioning through the media, religion, education, peer pressure, political correctness and cultural norms?

I have been hypnotized for most of my life, marching along in a trance. I have never enjoyed listening to the sound of society's humdrum anthem, yet for most of my life I tried to conform to its dictates all the same. However, I knew deep

2

within that I was not that which a blind society thinks I am, nor was I that which I might think I am. So, I decided to launch a deep investigation into the Truth of my Reality. I decided that I wanted to discover my true nature, beyond the thoughts and memories which I referred to as 'me'.

That investigation turned out to be a whirlwind adventure, traversing upon a long and winding maze like path. Along that path there were many detours, tangential issues and teachers of confusion to side-track me from awakening to what I wanted most sincerely - Reality, Truth, Spirit. Whatever name we give it, it is the same thing. It is realization of the ultimate Truth, the One actual Reality which rests beyond the individual thought world. When I asked myself that question, *"what am I?"* I began to suspect that I might be something I never even considered. I began to wonder that I might actually be something so unfathomable, that I couldn't even understand it with my thinking mind even if I tried to understand it.

So, after a long and unnecessary winding road of much philosophy, guru speech and sideshow new age issues, I finally awakened simply to the beauty, Oneness and Spirit of absolute Reality. Then 'I' came to realize, as far as limited words can explain, that 'I' and 'you' and everything else we perceive as being 'separate', are really One and the same. We are the same source manifesting as everything. We are that Reality which transcends all conceptual understanding. We are that which lives beyond the mind in absolute freedom. Many seers have called this unified Reality 'God', but I and many other finders of this Reality now call it the *One*, or simply Reality with a capital 'R'.

When this Truth began to dawn upon my awareness, I was somewhat cautious when it came to talking about it to others. My experience was showing me something which was proving hard to explain. How could I tell others that I was beginning to realize that we were all One and the same source as that which they referred to as being 'God'? How could I tell them that we were not separate from that Reality, and that we

3

actually were that? Furthermore, how could I tell people that they were not what they thought they were, and that all of what they considered to be their personality or 'me', was only ever thoughts playing tricks within their awareness?

This book is my attempt at tackling these questions. I have herein combined my two previous books *'Finding Reality'* and *'The Awakening of Spiritual Awareness'* into this one updated and expanded edition. I have done this to bring all of my writings into one place, simply to make it handier for the seeker of Reality.

Hopefully by the time you are finished reading, you will see clearly that we can choose if we desire it enough, to move through life as carefree as a light breeze, flowing in the moment with the One. Breathing easy and deeply, inhaling life like a connoisseur tastes wine, with every sense alive we can drink deeply all that life is, all that Truth is, and all that Reality is. We need no longer believe in the deceptive inherited lie, which the world has accepted as a substitute for Reality. We can turn our attention away from hypnotic dreamland; the home of the false mind made 'me', the self-imposed character of fiction (the ego). That ego weaves its tapestry of discord upon every mind, fraying the peace of the whole world, thereby eclipsing the spiritual Reality of us all.

I hope this book can help you to see that we are Spirit - the ever present One. We are the author of our grand illusion, yet we need not believe in what we have made, but can still fully enjoy this play called creation all the same. Each apparent individual may easily discover the Truth of this Reality, since that Truth is everywhere and within everything. Right here, right now, right where we stand there is the answer that holds spiritual freedom. Possibly when the human mind tires of its interest in playing a conceptual and theoretical game of life, and instead allows itself to *be* life, then Truth will dawn upon the shackled mind, burning away all that is not and awakening the attention to the All that is, that One undivided Reality which sets the Spirit free.

1

Once upon a time

The adventure begins:

Once upon a time, before I thought of myself as being a Truth seeker, I was in a real mess. My mind was a complete muddle and I didn't know a thing about how best to live my life. I certainly didn't have any sense of coherence or organized direction in life, and that's for sure. I recall that I would go around in a foggy daze, three quarters asleep, half dead and in an unending bad mood laced with paranoia. I had a collection of the dopiest fears, which when activated would make my rib cage quiver and my breathing become overwrought.

I was completely at the mercy of every mood swing, depression, craving and emotion that crossed my mind. Anyone could push my buttons with ease and get the desired reaction every time. In short, I was like a puppet that was unknowingly being dangled, controlled and manipulated by the strings of thought which I weaved mechanically within my mind – thoughts which I stupidly mistook for being 'me'.

Most of my thoughts were very dark, so as a consequence I felt despondent, yet I just wanted to be happy. I didn't think much during those days about anything else, apart from how wretched life appeared to be. I just couldn't see the point in life at all and I wanted to escape from it. Then one day, my mother came into the living room when I was resting, and she read out a passage from a spiritual book I had bought her for a Christmas present. The passage she read to me, as far as I recall, was along the lines of, *"Every thought is a prayer; you always get in your life, what you think about the most"*.

You know, that struck a small chord with me. My ears pricked up and I took notice, so to speak. So I read the passage for myself. Not only that, but I read the entire book, which was a bit unusual for me, since spiritual books didn't interest me at all back then, all of that spiritual stuff was my mother's interest, it certainly was not my thing. You see, I thought life was drudgery, with each day being the same as the one before, with nothing in the world appearing to have any meaning or objective, apart from dissolution of course.

I didn't realize back then, that it wasn't actually real life I was experiencing, but merely my own thoughts painted over life. I was blind to the Truth and was only bearing witness to my own thought projections. These thoughts, I unsuspectingly built upon every day, making my life experience each week more dire than the week before, and it would take the guts of ten years before I was willing to admit to myself that it was my very own thinking which was causing my deep displeasure with both myself and my life.

Of course I always thought that someone else was responsible for my mood swings; *"It's all his fault,"* I blurted on many an occasion. Life in general was out to get me; this could not be disputed in my mind during this time. For a time, I fooled myself into thinking that alcohol was a comfort, and I would get drunk almost five times a week to numb the boredom and darkness of my mundane existence. This of course would leave me feeling even more like a piece of trash. Life was a bit of a whirling misery go round for me back then, and I couldn't for the life of me see a way of getting off that whirling misery go round.

However, the spiritual book I began to read had a lot to say on the nature of life and the Self. It held a message about the peace and joy of Spirit we could have within our lives, if only we could tap into that Spirit. It was very interesting and it turned out to be the bait I would eagerly and voraciously bite upon, only to find myself launched into the exciting domain of the Truth seeker. The adventure had begun!

Six times I read this book, drinking in its wisdom. It spoke of enlightenment, a state in which one could commune directly to God. It promised that when I reached the state of union with God, I would therefore be protected and be immune to the big bad worlds onslaught. It painted God as being the universal source of all life; a unified intelligent energy which pervaded everything, and an energy which I was already One with. All I now had to 'do' was to become aware of this Oneness with God. So, apparently God wasn't an individual being who lived up in the sky, sitting upon a throne, busying himself throughout eternity with judging us all. Finally my naive belief in the story about the old bearded individual called 'god' had been done away with. That line from the Bible, *"In God we live and breathe and have our being"* then finally made some sense to me.

The promise of a fairy-tale happiness and a magical Kingdom of Heaven within my own being enlivened the cells of my entire body. I was awestruck. What this book I was reading promised was the complete opposite of the mundane existence I then endured as 'my reality'. My 'poor me' persona began coming apart at the seams upon hearing about the prospects of attaining this state of being called 'enlightenment'. That was my first step upon a ten year journey, on which I would investigate into all facets of spirituality; old, modern and alternative. This is when my life turned from being a misery go round, into a bit of a merry go round.

I kick started my spiritual adventure with meditation, as apparently, according to the book, this was the way to reach the state of enlightenment. Meditation brought me various strange experiences which I found difficult to understand. To get an explanation of the experiences I occasionally had, I read everything I could get my hands on about God, religion, meditation, philosophy and basically anything remotely sounding like a spiritual, philosophical, psychological or new age book. I devoured several hundred books during my spiritual search, like a starving wolf tearing its dinner to shreds. I just couldn't get enough. I spent over ten years like this, reading and listening to gurus, instead of just narrowing my focus down to the simplicity inherent within this awakened state which I was hearing all about.

Nevertheless, I finally had meaning to my life, and a direction. I became convinced that I was one of 'Gods' many right hand men. I now had a high and lofty purpose to my life. Because, don't you know, that when any self-respecting Truth seeker takes to the spiritual path, it is his personal responsibility to drag everyone else onto the path with him, even if they are having a great old time in life. Apparently people needed to be saved, and it didn't matter to me if their lives were hunky dory. They had to be saved from – eh, well - look it don't matter what they had to be saved from, right, they just had to be saved and that's the end of it.

Yes, one certainly had a mission to save the world, big place that it is. So, I was trying to get everyone about me to practice meditation, so they too could have a life of meaning and purpose, seeking for enlightenment or awakening, whatever name you wish to call it. It never struck me that maybe they were already chasing after their own supposed purpose, even if it was just a game in their imagination. I was so convinced that any purpose other than spirituality was a waste of time. Now that I had found this thrilling path, I felt like I had no other choice but to have others join me on it. And some did join me on it, eventually.

I surmised that if everyone I associated with was a Truth seeker like me, then we would all bring about Heaven on earth, or at least make life easier for each other. As a reward for my services, I was sure that 'God' would come rapping his heavenly energetic hand upon my door, with the state of enlightenment gift wrapped and bow tied like a juicy big present for me, his new best friend. I foolishly thought we would all end up enlightened together, spiritually awake and living our lives collectively in a modern day version of the Garden of Eden paradise. How wrong was I?

Spiritual highs and lows:

From the earliest years of my investigation, I heard all about how behind the scenes there was unity in all life, that indeed there was only One thing appearing as the many. I read about how this One thing was the same Source and Spirit that animated me, everyone and everything. Spiritual awakening was said to be a direct knowing perception of this One thing. The One was described in many ways, depending upon the teacher who was doing the describing. It was portrayed as being the Source of life itself, true abundance, joy, peace, God or the kingdom of Heaven etc. Knowing the Spirit within was said to be the same as knowing the Reality of everything, since everything was the One. Indeed, the One was said to be the only true Reality, and that humanity's dualistic perception of separation was a falsity. Many of the teachers claimed that words failed them, when trying to describe awareness of the One.

I eventually came to a point when I wanted this Reality more than anything else in life. I came to realize that I would forever remain a prisoner to dualism or separation, until I awakened in freedom to the spiritual Reality that is the One.

I had accumulated plenty of spiritual experiences throughout my seeking years, and yes, they were such a great old buzz. Nonetheless, towards the end of my ten year search, I was no longer interested in momentary spiritual experiences here and there, because experience is fleeting (here today, gone tomorrow). I figured that if spiritual experiences were going to tease me in this manner, then they were not worth having at all. They reminded me of a drug, where one could have a temporary high, only to end up chasing after the next high and be disappointed when you couldn't get it.

Now, admittedly, I was a very naïve young chap back then. I figured that awakening would be much like an endless state of euphoria, similar to a drug induced ecstatic state. I presumed that I could get my fix of spiritual awakening from a reliable spiritual guru, in the same manner as a junkie could get their fix of drugs from a reliable drug dealer. All I would have to do would be to find a good reliable dealer (guru) who could provide me with 100% of pure quality 'wisdom'. I would then cross his palm with gold and the dealer (guru) would dispense his wisdom. When I ingested the wisdom, I guessed that I would be readily able to shift into this trance like altered state of consciousness, and reside there buzzing in uninterrupted ecstatic spiritual bliss forever. I had heard that apparently life from that moment forth would contain no more problems, as I would be permanently reeling in a spiritual stupor.

However, this naïve belief was shaken, when I finally realized that momentary spiritual highs were not powerful enough to liberate me from the hypnotic spell of thought I was under. I wanted a complete and awakened freedom from being the puppet that was controlled by the strings of thought. Yet awakening still seemed to be so distant, even though I began to understand that it was only thought which maintained the illusion that blocked my awareness of Reality. On the other hand, I didn't fully understand that it was my willing and enduring investment in maintaining the thought constructed psychological 'me', which kept the hypnotic spell of thought firmly in place, saturating my awareness and blocking out Reality.

For a long time, until immeasurable frustration set in, I still sought the temporary spiritual highs as an alternative. I would get deluded, as I sought some way to make these experiences permanent. These experiences would occasionally fool me into believing that I was towing the right 'path'. Each time the experiences wore out however, I would feel disappointed and frustrated, wondering, *"What am I doing wrong here?"* This question led me to seek ever more voraciously, applying more and more effort. So I hunted down more gurus, books, methods, techniques and recipes for enlightenment in a desperate attempt at locating the answer to my quandary – finding a permanent freedom in Reality.

I chased mystical spiritual experiences every day for years, like a junkie chasing after his fix. It irritated me when I couldn't reproduce a certain state within my awareness. On the odd occasion when I would swat down a spiritual high, I'd say to myself, *"Yes, now I'm back on track"*. I would go and tell someone of my experience, but they would look at me like I was a weirdo, and anyhow, within a day or so, it would all be back again to square one; no spiritual high, still trapped in my dreams of thought, just me again, ordinary as I am.

Then it clicked with me, that maybe this was all a part of the problem. Could it be possible that I was using spirituality, merely as an escape from the ordinary right from the beginning? I was on a misery go round before I started upon the spiritual adventure and this is what I thought being ordinary was tantamount to – plain old misery. Now, you see what thoughts can do for ones outlook on life?

Everyone I looked upon was following the road of the ordinary. They looked like they were in a trance, and I didn't like what I *thought* the ordinary seemed to be leading us all to - a predictable, robotic and mundane existence all the way to the grave. I didn't want to follow the same old time worn path which everyone else seemed willing to blindly participate in. As a devout Truth seeker, I stupidly thought that I had to sacrifice the ordinary life scenario, before I could be spiritually awakened. So, as a result of my naive belief, I became very cynical about following an ordinary life.

My view of an ordinary life was - we are born and we go to school to receive indoctrination into how to join the society of the clones. We learn (unconsciously) how to be like everybody else, lest we get made fun of for being ourselves. If we rebel against this brainwashing, we are labelled uncooperative, non-conformist or trouble makers. And of course we may get labelled as being nerds or 'losers' by our so called 'friends' if we dare to be different. We leave school and maybe go on to university. After that we strive hard to get a 'good' job (that we possibly detest). Once the job is going 'well' we may get married, because we believe that we will live 'happily' ever after. Maybe we then have a few children, whom we can condition with societies clone like norms. Then as we progress through life we can retire to 'enjoy' ourselves whenever it is way too late, and then we're dead.

Back then, the ordinary life scenario always reminded me of the story of the Pied Piper I'd heard as a child. The Pied Piper (societies conditioned call) plays his whistle and all of the rats (humanity) follow behind him wherever he goes, in a hypnotic trance, with their minds asleep, dormant, nobody home and certainly nobody observant enough to assess the situation and awaken out of it. Anyone who dares to awaken from the hypnotic trance is laughed at, called a weirdo or a loony, verbally attacked and even possibly killed.

So, you might guess that I didn't have a very positive outlook. Thank goodness I've since been cured of that dreary outlook. However, back then, the ordinary life scenario, for some reason or other, wasn't enough for me during my spiritual search. It all seemed so lacking in any true and lasting meaning. I had to get to the bottom of what life was actually all about. I guess I was rather scientific in that regard.

I was one of those annoying guys, who at a party would kick start a good philosophical discussion, only to get too deep into it for most party goers. As a result, I would irritate people as I deconstructed and tore apart the fabric of the ego structured illusory reality. This never really went down very well. Over the years, I repeatedly noticed folks quickly leaving the room with a timid or glazed eye expression, whenever I got too deep into my self and world analysis. I think it usually frightened them, even though I thought it was very funny at the time. My attitude was - *Oh well, if I ever want to clear a room, at least I know what to start talking about.*

Though, perhaps I just thought a little bit too much for my own good back then. Is it any wonder I was so dissatisfied with ordinary life? If you are enjoying your ego structured altered reality, well what harm is there in it? It's just like being asleep and having a nice dream. Why would you want to awaken from a nice dream? You would only want to awaken if it was a nightmare, wouldn't you?

So what about you - are you having a nice dream?

Throwing in the towel:

However, there came a point when I began to understand that I was trying a little too hard to awaken, and as a result, I was beginning to feel frustration with my spiritual investigation. All this seeking was growing extremely tiresome for me. I also felt like I was becoming more reclusive. So I asked myself the question, *"What if I just left myself alone entirely and gave up searching for the extraordinary and the mysterious?"* Those momentary spiritual experiences I'd had were very nice, but considering that they never hung around for too long, or made that much of an impact upon my everyday life, I figured, why chase after them anymore? What if being ordinary (dare I say it) was okay after all?

In any case, if I did just become *present*, as most of the gurus were continuously and repeatedly suggesting that we seekers should do, maybe I would wake up quite casually and easily. If this was all I had to 'do' to find the freedom I sought, it would hardly matter a damn what kind of a lifestyle I lived afterwards. Once awakened in this easy manner, I was pretty sure I'd live a lifestyle in harmony with all of life anyway. I had heard enough awakened teachers stating that it is awakening which makes us truly sane and happy. So from that point of view, maybe I could actually get on with the business of an 'ordinary' life after awakening. After all, once that was taken care of, I would've already accomplished what I was born into

13

this world to do, the only purpose I felt that there really was, and that is to awaken to the true nature of Reality.

So being awakened, I figured that I wouldn't be causing any harm for myself or anyone else, since I would no longer be tolerating murky thoughts rattling around my head. So, I supposed I could just kick back, awakened in absolute freedom and enjoy the rest of the ride in whatever way that I wanted to. This sounded like a nice possibility, and just what I always wanted. However, then the alternate reality bell rang in my ear. Could I let all this seeking come to a complete end? Is there security in that final letting go? Am I sure that I don't need more knowledge; more guidance from teachers? I noticed that my thoughts were stuck to the old habit pattern of seeking, seeking and seeking. So, rather scientifically, I asked myself, what would happen if I did casually and effortlessly become present? How would using this observer mode of attention change things? What if I just united my attention with plain old life, just as it is?

As a result of 'doing' that, I supposed there would be no more manipulation from the thought made 'me'. There would be no more desire to control, or no more fighting against what I thought was not right. I would cease trying to make bad and awkward situations better. I would now finally be content with life to be just what it is, here and now, innocent, with no aspiration for the weird and the wonderful to occur. Would this finally leave me in freedom, awakened in union with the One which I desired?

One might guess, that after ten years of going around in circles, reading hundreds of books, seeking through the world after gurus, practicing possibly every meditation technique I ever heard of and setting aside ordinary life, a time would come when I would ask myself, *what for?* What was it all for? I felt like I was becoming honestly aware, maybe for the first time why I got into spirituality in the first place. I know I was having a dire time of it before I encountered the life of the Truth seeker, but I understood that I wasn't completely using spirituality as an escape mechanism.

I came to the knowledge, that there was most definitely something within me, propelling me on and on through all of the frustrations and searching. This something wanted to and needed to be given birth to. I then recalled from my early childhood, questioning myself on all kinds of strange topics that a child wouldn't normally be thinking about. What was I? Where was I? What am I even doing here, wherever here is?

I found life on Earth to be remarkably strange and well, dare I say it - *weird*. It appeared peculiar to be in this body, and seeing other people walking about the streets always reminded me of robots, programmed to play a role whilst oblivious to the hidden hand that operated them - the One (Spirit and Reality). Everybody looked like they were sleepwalking. We are so afraid of the idea of seeing a ghost, yet to my observations here are ghosts (Spirits) everywhere, on every street, dressed up in meat suits, mistaking the meat suit as being what they are, when in actuality they really are the One.

I remembered that as a child I would stare at my face in the mirror for long periods of time, and it just didn't stack up. That was not me looking back. That walking, talking, piece of meat was just not me. Something within me knew that this was all just an appearance, and the recognition of that was very, very strange indeed. Down through the years, I have had other people continuously remarking to me, rather casually, *"do you ever get the impression that we are all just dreaming this up?"* So I knew that it was not just me who noticed all of this, others did also. Although, perhaps they never felt the drive, like I did, to actually investigate it, to discover if the hunch was true.

This thing within me, craved to be born within my awareness. It had an extreme urgency throughout the last few months of my investigation. This haunting of Spirit, I felt, is why I could not settle for an 'ordinary' lifestyle. I queried the 'reality' of this whole existence here on Earth. I began to feel like life had no ultimate meaning, like someone was playing a big joke on us all. This once again, made the world appear very dark and pointless in my mind. I went back to feeling like a stranger in an inhospitable alien world.

So, right at that moment, more so then than at any other time, I wanted to find the One who was playing the big joke on us all. Deep down I had a feeling that all was not what it seemed to be, that this setup we were living was not real. I simply could not leave it at that by ignoring my deep hunch, only to pursue an ordinary life. Something within me wanted to wake up and make it-self known, and I realized that I could no longer get in its way.

Awakening:

Mere intellectual spiritual knowledge would no longer satisfy me because I would still be a prisoner, bound in the chains of philosophical and conceptual second hand knowledge. Spirit would be unable to express itself in my awareness due to that swirling mess of thought, casting its dark shadow like a cloud obscuring the sunlight. No, conceptual knowledge I had more than enough of. That conceptual search all ended up being a major part of the problem. I got totally bored with spiritual knowledge and all of the clever conceptualization that went with it.

I no longer wanted to talk to anyone about spirituality, as I didn't see the point anymore. Where once upon a time, I would enjoy getting involved in endless chatter about spiritual matters, I now felt that we might as well talk about the weather instead. I ended up seeing madness in humanity and within my own mind, which I was never aware of before, because my awareness was so caught up in being entertained by it.

I thought about this; *"If it is spiritual awakening that I want, then that Spirit is already within me".* This I knew for sure, due to all of those momentary spiritual experiences I had. I figured, *"Reality is then already the case, here and now, within me and all around me".* Then it clicked with me (recalling what some of the gurus had said), that it was simply a matter of where the focus of my attention lay. I realized that my attention was sleeping in dreamland. I was hypnotized with the silly, random and utterly nonsensical thoughts which passed through my awareness every minute. It was only when I shifted the focus of my attention out of those thoughts, like during meditation that I would find peace and spiritual experience arising within me.

When I allowed this shift to *Attentive Presence,* I would occasionally find myself erupt with laughter for no particular reason. This uncaused joy would spring up all on its own from deep within. I knew this was a quality of the Spirit when it was allowed to live in my awareness, unobstructed by thoughts. My breathing would even out, becoming very shallow and deeply relaxed. It was nice to experience this when I practiced meditation, but I wasn't satisfied with having this experience temporarily anymore. I got tired of using meditation as a sedative against the world's onslaught, which was impinging itself upon my personal reality more and more, as each week passed by. I needed a way of maintaining peace and dealing with the world head on, instead of running away or hiding from it.

Indeed, it seemed to be the case, or I don't know for sure, maybe I'm paranoid, but it appeared that every time I switched my attention from daydreams to Attentive Presence, people would throw craziness my direction for no reason that I could see. This of course would throw my mind into a spin again, as I got tricked into all of the complaining, explanations and judgements (thought dramas) which emanated from this. It felt like a big conspiracy, like there was some 'evil unseen entity' with a cunning plan to prevent my awakening. I was getting a little paranoid. If there was an 'evil unseen entity' placing negative obstacles in my way, then I have to thank that 'evil unseen entity', since it was the intensity of the trash I had to endure that made me want to awaken more so at that point than ever before.

Now of course, I realize that this 'evil unseen entity' stuff makes me sound like I'm a bit cuckoo, but I can't explain this any other way, as it did actually feel like something desperately wanted me to stay asleep in dreams, rather than awaken.

Maybe it was one of those illusive spirit guides we hear about, throwing challenges my way so I could turn to the Spirit through it all. If that was what it really was, then I was certainly not impressed with these apparent mischief makers. In fact, I figured that my spirit guides were not doing a very good job. I decided that they were a shower of schmucks. I figured that they must be drunk, laying slumbering in a backstreet alley of 'Heaven', with their head in a gutter, face down in a pool of their own puke instead of doing the job 'God' paid them to do, which was of course, to look after me. When I died, I resolved that I would go and hunt them down in 'Heaven' and then give each of them a good beating about the head and neck with a heavenly blunt instrument, for slacking off when they were supposed to be helping me.

Now, I would really like to blame a spirit guide or maybe even an 'evil unseen entity' for my woes back then, but I realized that it was the madness of my hypnotic thought that I was actually coming face to face with. I was becoming acutely aware of the trash thoughts which I had let take over my awareness every day. But for a time I was convinced that an unseen hand was ruining my life. Now that I am willing to admit the truth, I guess that my spirit guides can finally breathe a sigh of relief, now that I've let them off the hook.

Nevertheless, admitting that I was to blame for my woes was disheartening, soul destroying and I hate to use the religious term, but it was reminiscent of the 'dark night of the soul'. Except of course, in my case, it was more like a dark year of the soul. I was thinking some very dire thoughts during this period and I believed them all to be absolute truth. This I realized, was all due to a remaining yet small reluctance, to let go of the mind made 'me' (hypnotic thought identity) and to defend that false identity at all costs. My own thinking was the only real enemy or 'evil unseen entity' there ever had been in my life.

When the realization dawned that awakening was all up to me and me alone, and did not depend upon my exterior circumstances improving, I decided that I was done with the delay tactics and excuses I used to remain asleep in dreamland. I then kick started the last battle for my sanity; a spiritual war for my Reality. I was finally ready and willing, to let everything I thought I was and everything I thought I knew go completely. I realized that I didn't really have to 'do' anything concerning effort whatsoever. I could not seriously call Attentive Presence 'doing', since it was more a case of undoing rather than of me actually 'doing' anything.

By shifting my attention fully into the present, I noticed that I was no longer caught up in the thought dramas. The more I allowed Attentive Presence to take hold, the more I found the old daydreaming habit loosening itself, and its momentum was becoming somewhat weaker. At first there was a bit of a see-saw effect going on within my awareness, as I was going backwards and forwards between daydreams and Attentive Presence (Reality). However, I understood that whether or not I stayed in Reality or thought dramas, depended solely on the weight of my desire. Like breaking any old habit, if we really and truly want to break the habits we hold, then the weight of our desire to break those habits is crucial. I discovered that the necessary desire came from my state of readiness. This is when I reached a tipping point and finally found myself ready and willing to let thought dramas go completely.

If we have a big weight of readiness behind our desire for awakening, then soon we will develop a new habit-momentum of Attentive Presence naturally. This is when awakening becomes easy. I finally had a big weight of willingness behind my desire to awaken, and I found this to be the key ingredient when it came to awakening. And so, I allowed myself to switch into Attentive Presence without wishing to manipulate or control the outside world's infringements upon my life. This allowed for my awakening to Reality. Now, staying awake in Reality has overtaken the old momentum of daydreaming.

The awakening itself felt very much like being reborn. Due to my see-sawing back and forth for a little while, the realization gradually grew stronger in my awareness with each day, and then it progressively took over. A sudden explosive awakening was not my experience.

The world then transformed back into the world of crystal clear clarity which I knew of as a child. However, it appeared brighter than I remembered it. Everything was appearing to be more real, pristine, new and fresh, full of magic and wonder. Everything was alive, even inanimate objects, and all things seem to be aware of my wakeful presence, like I have stumbled upon a great secret. I now live with a constant undercurrent of ease, peace, and contented joy. Often the body feels almost weightless and energetically charged. There is to varying degrees, feelings of electricity or energy, mildly tingling and sometimes pulsating through the body. There is an immense sensation of what can only be described as peaceful freedom.

As I look upon the world around me, I sense that I am looking at myself (not the body or thought made egoic 'me') but something else, which I can only call the One, since everything is unified. There is a sensation a lot of the time that is like a blending or a dissolving into the air and everything around me. What accompanies this realization is the experience that I am (at base level) all that I gaze upon, and that in actual Reality there is no separation between anyone or anything. I recognize first hand that the body and the thought made egoic 'me' (the entity called Keith Loy), never did have any absolute truth to it. When this realization is at its strongest, it feels very much like entering a Void and being stripped bare, or emptied of all sense of individuality. Yet the funny thing is, that although everything is experienced as unity (the One); there is also retained a sense of an observant entity or Spirit. I call this observant entity the

Spirit because no other word in my vocabulary will suffice. So, a unity and a seeming duality all at the same time; a paradox, is it not? I guess this is why a lot of awakened guys say that the awakening cannot be expressed accurately in words.

Now, some teachers will state that there is 'nobody' that needs to be awakened. Well, the realization I have encountered is as stated, that the thought made 'me' and indeed the physical body are not an absolute truth. However, there is this observant conscious awareness, and I have discovered that it is this observer which shakes off the hypnotic spell of daydreams and thought dramas. This observer becomes aware of itself. Consciousness realizes its essential pure nature. This observer is non-local but it is also localized in awareness as a witnessing presence. This Spirit or observing conscious awareness is what we really are. It's nature is Unity or Oneness, yet it plays the game of apparent duality also. We are this One no-thing; this observing awareness. So, although some teachers say there is 'nobody' home that needs to be awakened, there most definitely is a something home!

However, this awakened realization is not a fixed state. This fluctuates mildly to varying degrees within the awareness. It's sometimes more pronounced and at other times not so pronounced. Although, the Oneness and contented peace is always there whenever we lose all interest in dreamland and its thought dramas, which is the only thing that can ever really block out that Unity and contented peace.

2

Attentive Presence

Are you ready for now?

I found that the readiness to allow awakening to occur had to be in place, before momentary spiritual experiences could mature into what has been called 'awakening'. One cannot force this readiness, since it is either there or it is not there. Readiness arises as we find ourselves willing to loosen our grip and demand upon the moment. It is a state of non-attachment to the outcome, when we learn to take life as it comes. I discovered over the years that most seekers were really only interested in being believers, and in gaining entertainment through seeking. Many devoted their lives to a philosophy, a belief system or a 'spiritual' practice, but most 'seekers' had absolutely no readiness at all to allow an absolute shift within their awareness from dreamland to Reality.

And this is all awakening really amounts to. Once you are totally ready to flow with life as it is, it only requires a mere shift of the attention from the thought world to the Real world. There are no beliefs or improvements needed, no battling with sin or past hurts, no divine graces, no trumpets sound and there's no spiritual fireworks either. It is quite an ordinary thing, whenever we are willing to see beyond our insistence that it is something which will be forever out of reach and beyond us. It is always readily available, here and now, to anyone who truly desires it. But because the world believes that it is like some kind of drug induced high, we find that many in the world remain as seekers and never finders.

Awakening brings pure clarity, peace, freedom from mental turmoil and awareness of our natural spiritual state in union with life. Various internal spiritual experiences will come and go *naturally*, but one is no longer attached to, or driven by the desire for spiritual experiences any longer. One is then driven by the pure desire for Oneness and absolute mental freedom.

Awakening arises within the awareness as a response to our willingness, unyielding desire and readiness to allow the present moment to be *just as it is*. There is a sense of surrender which happens when the mind casually gives up its perpetual manipulation and control. This usually occurs when we tire of the stress and effort which mental control brings. If we are always trying to contort our everyday 'reality', or find ourselves making attempts at trying to 'become' a better 'me', then we are not allowing life or Reality to be as it is; we are interfering with life's natural flow. Awakening happens when we stop battling against our natural self, and when we quit berating ourselves for not being 'spiritual' or 'good' enough. It happens when we stop insisting that we have a troubled past which is torturing us, because the reality is that there is <u>no past,</u> until we ourselves bring up a thought of the past in our mind.

Awakening happens when we finally understand, that this present moment is the only moment which really matters, it is the only moment that is *real*, and it is the only moment where life in all its fullness takes place. Right here in the now of any and every moment, we can find our freedom from the prison house of thought drama. With every seeming <u>mundane</u> moment we are given an invitation to wake up to the true nature of our Reality. Right here, right now, you too could allow awakening to occur if you were only ready to step outside the mind and embrace life, just as it arises before you, with no more egoic demands being made upon the Reality of now.

23

Attention to the present is the key to mental and spiritual freedom. If it were not for the many conflicting and confusing teachings which surround spiritual awakening, many more honest seekers throughout the world would have awakened with ease, fairly early on in their search.

Yet, although awakening is approached in an ordinary kind of way, its effect can also be at times breath taking. The sense of pure liberation and lack of restriction which arises as a result of the awakening of spiritual awareness is revolutionary to the sense of the individual 'me' which feels isolated and separate from everyone and everything. Our perception is then transformed with a sense of unity or a blending with all of life. Then a true understanding of the term 'all is One' finally becomes clear, whereas maybe beforehand it was only an intellectual belief or a theoretical hypothesis.

What should we do?

Some teachers tell us that we have to 'do' this or 'do' that in order to awaken to our true nature. This of course gives rise to effort. But surely there is no actual 'doing' required to merely shift our attention into Reality. Obviously we have to 'do' something to cover up or distort our awareness of what is real, do we not? So then, what are we doing to block out awareness of our Reality? Have a look within your mind and you should have no problems in answering that question. Where is your attention? Are you being attentive to Reality (the present moment) at all, or are you lost within the dreamland you carry around inside your head? When we look at dreams, then all we see is dreams. When we look at Reality, then all we see is Reality.

In order to be aware of anything, then we have to give our attention over to whatever it is that we wish to be aware of. To bring realization of Reality into awareness, we have to give our attention over to what is *real*, and divert our attention away from what is un-real. Since no real 'doing' can possibly be required to be in alignment with Truth, then awareness of Truth cannot possibly be a difficult or hard thing to be aware of. What effort or exertion could really be required in being true to our natural selves, and in being true concerning the expression of that natural self within the world? Exertion lye's only in fighting against the natural self, not with being in alignment with it.

Many sincere Truth seekers misunderstand the do 'nothing' talk we hear from various teachers. They will take it quite literally, and then end up with a mind full of second hand philosophy, and as a result, they may forever remain un-awakened. Is it any wonder people get confused by this? They are told to do 'nothing' by many teachers, and they don't fully grasp that by shifting their attention to the *Real*, then that is actually how the mind ceases its constant and never ending doing. Now a shift of attention cannot in any way be considered to be an act of 'doing'. We do not have to 'do' something to shift our attention from one thing to another. A shift of attention is not a strenuous art form which requires lots of practice. It only takes an honest willingness for it to happen, and obviously we have to fully want the awakening to happen also. Many people say that they do want to awaken, but when you really listen to them and the many excuses they make to remain asleep, you will find that they don't *really* want to awaken. And why is that? Well, because there is no trust that the Spirit will make things better for them.

There is a deep fear of letting go of the control which the ego exerts. Now, we should all realize that awakening does require trust that the Spirit will enliven our being far more than we could ever think possible. The trust required is similar to that trust you would need just before making a bungee jump. Awakening is exactly like a bungee jump into unknowingness. We have to trust that we are being held securely, and that we won't falter through allowing the awakening of spiritual awareness.

25

We are afraid to let go fully, because we tend to think that through the thought content of our mind, we can give our lives some meaning, but our lives will never have any true meaning until we awaken to Truth. The 'meaning' which thought appears to give our lives is always very short lived. When our egoic 'meaning' fizzles out we usually end up wondering where all of the magic went to, as we lament the past and yearn for it to return to us. The ego will keep us brooding over of the past, or else fearing the future. We even allow ourselves to get sad about our good memories, because we cannot relive them *now*. By doing this we are ignoring our present and the result will be that we will one day lament this present moment also, because we never fully lived it whilst it was happening.

We usually don't embrace the moment fully at all, since we believe that nothing is really happening right now which is worthy of our attention. We lock our attention up in a prison house of thought drama, instead of embracing the now of life. We might as well have a television on inside our heads, to entertain ourselves all day long, because that is exactly what most of us having running in our mind most of the time - *dramas*, the likes of which you would see on the television. The only difference being of course, that the dramas we run in our mind we mistake for reality, whilst the dramas on television, we know are not real.

However, by doing this, we might as well just stay in bed in the morning and roll over to go back to sleep, so we can dream a few more dreams. We aren't really living at all. We're being lived through by mechanical thought. We are possessed by thought, and our true nature is lost to our awareness whilst we remain possessed like this.

The one thing which the ego will not tolerate is the present, because in the present the past and future no longer exist. We can only really beat ourselves up mentally, when we allow our attention to fall asleep within the illusion that is the 'past' or 'future'. For example; when you get sad, what are you getting sad over? It is a memory of something that has

26

happened in the recent or distant past, isn't it? Memory is thought and with Attentive Presence you go beyond thought, and therefore the source of your sadness. Or maybe you have allowed your thoughts to drift into the illusion of the 'future' and now you feel sad. Perhaps because you have lost hope over something you wanted to happen in the future, and now it looks like it might not work out the way you planned after all. Once again, the future is thought and when you go beyond thought, then you go beyond all of your mental woes.

The ego mind teases us with this mental nonsense, and that's why most of the world remains stuck in their past. Most folks get to a certain age, and then they are always found to be telling the tales of yesteryear, whilst believing that the good times have past them by, and now all they have to look forward to is getting old and merely existing from day to day, no longer really living life with passion.

This need not be the case though. This is the way the ego lives, but the awakened live in a very different manner. The awakened are free from the egos boring tiny world, they are free from its dictates, its system of conformity, its rules and regulations and its constant rehashing of the past. If we truly seek for this kind of freedom, then we need to trust in our Spirit, and let go of the steering wheel in our mind. We need to jump into Reality, just like a free fall, and we need to enjoy the ride, because it certainly is a whirlwind adventure.

The effort of becoming:

There really is no effort required in this whole business of awakening. When we have had our gut full of the ego mind and its thought spell, then awakening is the easiest thing in the whole wide world. It's like a tipping of the scales, where more weight finally shifts over to the awakening side of the scales, than there was on the dreaming side. But if on some level we don't actually *want* to let go of our thought dramas, then we may try to convince ourselves that awakening is indeed a difficult thing. But you know, it is only ourselves we will be fooling, and only our own time and money we will be wasting as we run around buying numerous books and visiting various teachers. Those who are ready for awakening will awaken, and those who want to remain asleep will stay asleep, despite declaring themselves to be Truth seekers.

These types aren't really Truth seekers at all; what they are is entertainment seekers. Listening to the guru becomes exactly like watching an interesting movie on the television. They listen to the gurus' words and then turn what he has said into a set of beliefs (like hypnosis). No harm in that I suppose, it could make for a nice little dream. It's a pity though; being exposed to the teachings of Truth and then ignoring it all, simply because you are treating the teacher like he is some sort of stand-up spiritual entertainer.

The seeker, who wants to stay in the thought dream, usually settles for getting involved in a whole lot of effort; what has become known as the effort of becoming. It's like a game we might play with ourselves. Really it's the old performance of trying to sound like, look like, and act out the behaviour patterns of what we think a spiritual person should behave like. The spiritual stereotype is what I call it. This never leads to awakening though, even if we somehow manage to fight tooth and nail against our true nature, and to some extent manage to keep this so called 'spiritual' act going 24 hours a day. This performance is just another way of trying to alter our personality, so we can be accepted – maybe this time by 'God'. It operates as a major blockage to discovering the Truth, since this performance is not in line with Truth. This is a lie which we are persistently upholding, and lies act like clouds which obscure the sunlight of Truth.

To be aware of Spirit, we do not need to run around like a spiritual stereotype saintly figure, with a make-shift halo floating above our heads, most certainly not, because that would not be real. Many honest seekers get caught up in the effort of trying to become a stereotype of what we think 'spiritual' is supposed to look like. But trying to become something other than what we actually are is once again interfering with our Spirits true natural expression.

Now, the Spirit will never express itself in a bad way, only thought will do that. Spiritual stereotypes are the produce of thought, they come from sources which we gather from outside of our true being; usually from laws and rules conjured up by a religion, or possibly an egoic teacher. But don't you see that the Truth is not a lie – it is a Truth!

Trying to force ourselves to fit into someone else's' picture of how we should be behaving is restricting, and it requires for us to operate a major censor within ourselves. Now, restriction and censorship are not ingredients which give rise to the birth of spiritual freedom, most certainly not. Freedom comes only when we see clearly the hypnotic grasp which thought holds upon our awareness, and we then recognize thought for the illusion that it is, and as a result of that clear seeing, we decide to move beyond thought and into Reality instead. So restriction and censorship give birth only to *slavery* and not freedom. Therefore, trying to mould our behaviour in an effort to put on a performance of the spiritual stereotype is exactly like a willing slavery. This takes an awful lot of energy, and it stands as a major blockage before realization of the Truth.

But heh, this effort of becoming, at least it can become our new hobby, since it keeps us busy with a forever task, which we will never ever fully master. It reminds me of playing Golf. Golf is a game even the best say you can never fully master, but many will still die trying, rather than just giving up and enjoying the game, *as it is.* So, trying to become something that you are not, will never win out at the end of the day either; it'll just stress you out and ruin your enjoyment of life. But as we all know, some like the stress game, even if it ruins their enjoyment of life. So, the effort of becoming is an interesting little game we can play to try altering our true self, so we can 'become' what we think we should 'become' - a new thought made spiritual looking 'me'.

I have a question for you. Spend some time considering the ramifications of this question as it relates to your identity. Ask yourself now, and wait for an answer - *Am I, what I think I am?*

Awakening is nothing more than a clear seeing of all that we are not, and a direct realization of what we truly are. It is a clear seeing of life as it is. It is a pure awareness that we are One thing appearing as everything. We are that pure energy, Spirit or consciousness which gives birth to our life, world and universe. Thought borrows energy from this pure source to create a substitute for our true nature. From memories based upon past conditioning and life events, we automatically create 'me' as we drift along through life. It is like a computer program which we are constantly updating. But all of this is just thought rattling around inside our head. This is what we use to meet the world with.

We do indeed have a naturally wired genetic character to play the game of life, but because our natural character maybe isn't in line with the silly stereotypes of the world, we begin to feel like something isn't right with 'me'. So we begin to act out the part of how we think we should be, lest someone criticises us or makes fun out of us. We usually end up suffocating our natural self as we fight to become, become and become. And all the while whilst we are doing this, we are putting up invisible barriers to awareness of our true natural self.

Now, if we could only cease this endless cycle of becoming, by embracing who and what we naturally are; not what we think we are, or what we think we have to be; then ease, peace and the flowing river of life will reveal itself to smooth our way in this world. The way will then be left open finally, for true awakening to occur.

Attentive Presence:

Now, attention to the present moment is the key to awakening. I simply call it Attentive Presence. With Attentive Presence we become simple minded, not docile or stupid; it's just that our mind becomes clear and free from the burden of fixed thought patterns and we are simple, living life in the moment. Some have tried to turn this into a technique but it is not a technique, since children are mainly living in this mode quite naturally, as we too once were. Perhaps you remember it?

However, as we grow older and the world closes in around us, it usually leaves us in a mode of being where we end up thinking more about life, rather than truly living life in the present. Therefore, the present usually eludes us as we spend our time thinking, thinking and thinking. Attentive Presence brings an end to the thought spell, and leaves us awakened to our true spiritual nature, free in life and in spiritual Oneness.

A rolling stone gathers no moss, they say. Well, with Attentive Presence you will no longer gather any moss (thought dramas) within your mind, and no moss of thought shall stick to your awareness any longer. You'll be free to flow through life, fully enjoying your true natural character. No longer will the effort of becoming taunt you.

Once you know that you fully desire awakening, and realize that you are indeed worthy of it; when you trust that the Spirit can brighten your life better than the psychological 'me' (ego) could ever do, then you can finally make that definite decision to awaken, and live your life with Attentive Presence in Reality.

So, let's define Attentive Presence a little clearer. Let's get a little technical here just for a moment. Throughout my years as a seeker it used to irritate me greatly whenever I heard teachers talk about living in the present moment. Why did I get irritated? Well, because they would leave you high and dry, and never go into the particulars of how one was actually supposed to join their attention with the present moment.

They would of course blather about how it was not something one could 'do', and that we have no choice as to whether it happened or not, because there is 'no-one' there to make a choice. Of course, this made me want to yawn, yawn and yawn. Hence, I always found myself getting mildly irritated with all this guru talk. Yet, I have never understood a mere shifting of attention as being an act of 'doing'. Anyway, what follows is the simplicity of shifting your attention away from thought dramas and into Reality instead, in a way that possibly a child could understand.

Come to your senses!

You've heard that before, haven't you? There's nothing new here for you then, is there? Or could you possibly believe that this is far too simple to be effective for awakening to Reality? Well, who said life had to be complicated anyway, perhaps life is simple after all? Anyway, let's go into that a little deeper, just in case you don't understand what 'coming to your senses' actually means.

In order to be Attentive to the present Reality, then we have to realize that the Reality we are seeking for is here and now, within us and all around us. So, we have to perceive that Reality in the only way that we can perceive, and that is through each of our five senses. If we shift our attention *fully* to whatever we experience here and now, in each of our senses, then our mental awareness has not got any room left over to be sleeping in the dreamland of thought dramas, thus we shake off the dreamland and wake up to Reality. If we are doing anything at all, for example, driving the car, working, reading, washing up, playing sports, gardening, walking, listening or talking, eating, watching the T.V (in short, anything), then keep your full attention in your senses, without the inner thought commentary!

This is pure experiencing, and it allows for us to encounter an uncluttered, wakeful and alert pure awareness.

Start with what you hear, then maybe move on to what you feel, see, smell, taste – go around your senses drinking in all that life has on offer, getting out of your head and being fully attentive to the present.

Then when ones awareness is kept clear of the thought traffic, one begins to perceive Reality through the eyes of the Spirit. This is when we will stumble upon the present spiritual Reality we have been ignoring, possibly for all of our lives. However, we should make no demands upon what we *think* we should experience; we simply kick back, united with life as it is, savouring and appreciating like a connoisseur the moment that is now.

Thoughts will still come and go, but this is what we should *allow* them to do - to come and go. We certainly should not allow ourselves to get caught up in any daydream scenarios or thought dramas. We simply wake our attention out of its sleep, and allow ourselves to become attentive to life as it is; to let our attention bypass any daydreams or thought dramas that may be running in our mind. Soon we will find that the hypnotic spell of thought is broken, and our attention is awakened with the new wakeful momentum of Attentive Presence instead, hence the popular word spiritual seekers use – *Awakening!*

Maybe, if we so desire it enough, we will allow the new habit of Attentive Presence to become our way of life, since it is our natural state or mode of operating anyway. Being caught up in thought dramas and make believe worlds is not natural, even if you enjoy it. By allowing the habit of Attentive Presence the Real world opens up to you, and that my friend is a finer place to live in.

I hope you are beginning to recognize now, that we do not have to try to become 'spiritual', since spiritual is already our true Reality, even if we remain unaware of that truth right now. You, as you are, are in a perfect position for awakening, if you could only desire Reality more than dreamland. Then you will realize that spiritual freedom can be right now, in Reality.

You will realize that awakening is about choosing the freedom of Reality, instead of being a slave to our thought processes.

If we could only give up searching for the extraordinary; for the weird, the wonderful and the mysterious. If we would only come to our senses, attentive to the present, uniting our attention with life, just as it is, then we would find much to our surprise that the mystery which we have been seeking for all along, will no longer be a mystery!

3

The Thought World

The 'spiritual' thought world:

I have discovered that in the mind of some Truth seekers, awakening is perceived to be a difficult thing to allow within ones awareness. However, I have now reached the conclusion that some of those who believe awakening to be difficult don't really hold this belief due to a lack of understanding, but rather, they believe it simply because they *want* to believe it. Some don't really want to take responsibility for their own awareness, because taking responsibility for your own awareness means that we have to stop playing the victim game. We have to cease blaming everyone and everything else for our own neurotic thinking.

The belief in awakening being difficult also makes for a good excuse to keep the seeking game alive. It tends to lock one into a nice and fluffy little 'spiritual' thought world – a world of belief, a world of philosophy, a world of talk and a world where we seek and do not find. Indeed, you would find that if you were to *actually* awaken, then it is considered to be politically incorrect to even mention it to anybody. Claiming to be awake is considered to be an egotistical thing to be doing. Many 'spiritual' teachers won't even admit to being awake, merely because of this taboo. But why do we hold that attitude though?

Some might say, that it is because at our centre there is no-one or no 'me' to become awakened. So claiming to be awake is then viewed as being rather pointless. However, this seeming non-dual talk, I've noticed, only makes for more head stuff to trap one within a maze of thought (the thought world). This type of philosophy only fills the mind with confusion, and let's face it; when it comes to awakening there is a world of confused teachings out there already. Philosophy of this nature keeps seekers talking and *thinking* eternally about awakening, and the end result is usually no awakening. Dare I say it, but I feel that the taboos reserved for those who claim to be awake are just ego tactics, to keep awakening forever mysterious, unusual and at bay, so the world can remain sound asleep and undisturbed within its dreams of 'spiritual' thought, with no annoying awakened guys pulling back the curtains announcing, *"Waky waky, the night is over and the sun is up, dream time is over. Now is the time to rise and shine"*.

These taboos keep the 'spiritual' thought world firmly in place. It keeps us all philosophizing, believing and thinking about spiritual matters, without ever awakening out of the 'spiritual' thought world and coming to life in the present Reality of Spirit, as it is exists, here and now. We should realize that many seekers want to keep seeking and to *never* find, as strange as it may seem. The 'spiritual' thought world can be thrilling and fun, and whilst we find our 'spiritual' thought world to be thrilling and fun, well then, I guess we just won't find enough desire within ourselves to step out of that 'spiritual' thought world, to embrace the simple wonder of presence.

So, we will find some folks latching onto any old philosophy, belief or excuse at all, just so they can remain asleep in the 'spiritual' thought world. The 'spiritual' thought world makes for a nice pastime or hobby to fill one's life with. Those who treat the teachings of awakening in this manner will always insist upon awakening being difficult and requiring lengthy spiritual searches.

Now, the reason why some folks *believe* that awakening is difficult, is simply because, unconsciously they know that their manufactured thought identity (ego) would then begin to unravel. After spending a lifetime building up an identity made of thoughts, it could be misperceived that some great sacrifice is being made in order to let that thought based 'me' go. But it can hardly be considered to be a sacrifice to let go of something as shabby as the ego, in order to awaken to that which is *Real*. Although, because we have possibly forgotten what being in tune with the Spirit is like, we prefer to think that our 'spiritual' thought world and our dreams of 'me' are far more stimulating than our true spiritual nature.

Well, who would you be without those never-ending daydreams, huh?

The commentator:

The ego doesn't want to let the mind settle down, and it wants to keep at bay what it perceives as being emptiness or 'boredom'. This is why the ego loves philosophy or the 'spiritual' thought world. This all gives the mind something to latch onto, and it usually keeps the false sense of a separate 'me' intact, whilst the hypnotized entity believes that he or she is on a path to spiritual freedom.

You see, the ego perceives the peaceful mind as being devoid of any stimulation. Indeed, the ego thinks that peace is *boring*. The ego is constantly interpreting life through thought. It is like having your own personal commentator inside your head, making remarks and telling stories as you go about your day, trying to live your life in 'peace'. Yet all the while, we think that the cause for our lack of peace lies outside of us, but really that cause lies within our own thinking. The inner commentator is always telling us what life is like, and if it is telling us upsetting stories, then we perceive life to be upsetting; hence our peace is disturbed. The commentator is always trying to tell us who we are, what others are like and what life itself is like. Thoughts, thoughts and more thoughts; at all times we have this commentator hypnotizing us with its content. So all that we ever *really* perceive is a thought world, and rarely ever do we experience the *Real* world.

The thought commentator can be very much like one of those boring television news presenters, who enjoys spicing up a meagre story with a whole lot of lies, just so the viewing public will tune in to hear the 'shocking' news. Nelly Sleepwalker who lives in dreamland will say to her friend, *"Heh, did you hear what the man on the news said; the world's going to hell in a hand basket"*. As Nelly Sleepwalker and her friend believe this 'news', they will find themselves living out their lives based upon it all. Yet all the while they are being fed lies. Just like the boring news presenter who comments upon simple life as if something major is always occurring, the thought commentator in our mind does the very same thing with its never ending thought dramas.

Now, imagine if no thought dramas rattled around our awareness. What if we began to ignore the inner commentator of thought, and decided to live our lives in a pure perceptual manner, without referring perpetually to the commentator in our heads? Now, that's a really *big* question, because we would then have to evaluate just how important or entertaining we find the commentator to be. Do we have enough trust in the Spirit to fire the commentator and hire the Spirit instead? Most of us spin these thought dramas in our mind for the entertainment they provide, much in the same way as Nelly Sleepwalker likes to obtain her entertainment from watching the 'shocking' news. The ego thrives on these thought dramas, even if they cause us to feel like we are living in a nightmare.

So, the ego perceives the relinquishment of its thought dramas as being a sacrifice. Without the inner entertainment, it does actually believe that the peace of mind which will ensue is tantamount to a boring stagnation. Of course, one who is lost in egoic consciousness may not realize, that far from being boring and stagnant, the emergence of Spirit within ones awareness fills one with a sense of abundance, true happiness and authentic peace.

Now, to allow awakening to take hold, all we would be 'doing' is diverting our attention away from the internal entertainment and out into Reality instead. When we 'do' this, or rather, when we *allow* this, we will be freeing the Spirit, thereby allowing it to flow unencumbered throughout the body and mind. This freeing of the Spirit from the prison of thought would enliven ones perception, mind and everyday life to such an extent, that even the most positive of egoic daydreams would pale in comparison. But there is very little trust on the part of the ego, to believe that the Spirit could do a better job than it does. So we keep our hands gripped firmly upon the steering wheel of our mind, ever fearful to even *dare* to let go, and surrender to the flow of life instead.

Furthermore, there is a fear which is held that awakening brings ego annihilation. Now, this fear is even logically understandable, since the ultimate in spiritual realization brings an experience of what can only be termed as being a Void or emptiness. This experience is the ultimate stripping away of all character references, of all sense of 'me', of all individuality and of all everything. This is why I use the word Void, simply because this word describes it closer than any other, but words will never really describe this experience. And the Void experience is just that - an experience. Like all spiritual experiences, it comes and goes; it never hangs around for long, since it would be impossible to operate in that state. However, there is no annihilation as such, but the ego thinks that there is. It is always trying to fill up this perceived emptiness with thought.

With awakening to your true nature comes realization that the psychological 'me' (ego) who we believe ourselves to be, is nothing more than a phantom. In Reality it doesn't even *exist,* and the body will be seen clearly as being a vehicle for the Spirit to play the game of life on Earth. So the fear of the ego (thought identity) to face its own non-existence, and the realization that it is only an appearance in thought, which we have hypnotically given our belief over to, is most intolerable for most folks to even want to hear about, never mind consider.

In truth, the thought identity (ego) which you have been building up all of your life is like a mirage. All that you have ever considered to be 'you' is a lie. Everything you have ever told 'yourself' about yourself; all of your fears and all your little hang-ups are all lies, and have not one bit of truth to them. Everything you say you are and everything you have ever considered to be 'you' was only ever thoughts playing tricks in your mind. Thoughts weaved dreams inside your awareness, and quickly took the throne where your true spiritual nature should be sitting. The Spirit is your Reality and thought identity (ego) is an imposter. It maintains its illusion through mental effort, and acts much like a vampire, sucking on your spiritual energy in order to maintain this deception. Everything it says is 'me' is always changing with no permanence at all, so how can that be real?

Rather than awaken, some seekers would rather get lost in any tangential 'spiritual' issue, simply because they find the 'me' to be extremely entertaining. However, one can spend a lifetime chasing after gurus and having spiritual 'experiences', yet still remain completely asleep and hypnotized by the commentator and its fictional character called 'me'. The reason for this, is simply because of an un-willingness to allow the shift of attention from thought to Reality to occur within the awareness.

When I allowed awakening to occur, I could then perceive the absolute madness which the psychological 'me' (ego) was composed of. I realized that I had emerged from a mad dream, and I could then see others around me, still very much hypnotized with that dream. Some didn't even want to hear that there was a way out of the dream, or that there could possibly be a better way. I observed how some seemed to relish this madness, with absolutely no desire to ever let it go. Everyone appeared to want the dream over Reality. At first this was somewhat perplexing. This awakening business wasn't at all what I formerly imagined it to be. The gurus didn't tell me that it would feel much like you were only one of a few awake, within a world full of sleepwalkers.

Thought contamination:

So what causes the madness? What causes one to sleepwalk through life? Well, for the average person, their awareness is usually filled with junk thoughts, leaving no room within the awareness for anything else to be realized, never mind Reality and the One. Consider that the average person's awareness is like a room, which has been stuffed with a whole lot of old junk. You can barely move in that room, due to the collection of old junk you are hoarding in there. Well, the junk in this room is comparable to all of those little thoughts, which are rattling around the average person's awareness. When we have our mind filled up with junk thoughts, well then, all we are aware of is the nature of these thoughts. A room which has been filled to its capacity with junk, doesn't have any space left in it for anything else, does it? And neither will your awareness have any room left over to be aware of anything else, whilst you have it filled with junk thoughts.

Hence, we will be living in a thought world and not the Real world. You see, if your awareness is crammed with thoughts all the time, then what actually happens is that you look out *through* these thoughts and into the world, thinking to yourself, "*This is the way the world is*". So all you really get to see is the world according to the nature of the junk you have lurking inside your mind.

People are hypnotized with thoughts, which they consider to be absolutely true. Through thought we create enemies for ourselves, whenever there may be nobody actually threatening us or doing us any harm at all. We create belief systems and philosophies, and these contaminate our pure awareness so much, that we dare not even call them into question. We allocate fears and other identifications to ourselves, so we can have a fictional 'me' to parade in front of

41

our friends. But this is all mere thought, and we allow ourselves to become spellbound by it.

Everyone is an actor they say, and this is what you get to see whenever you finally allow awakening to happen. It could be quite startling to observe someone who is putting on an act for you, just because they want you to perceive them as the 'me' whom they like to think they are. It's a bit like being in the twilight zone. Some people like to think of themselves as being the tough guys, or some believe themselves to be shy and introverted, yet others try their damndest to be the centre of attention, but it's all just thought projected out and into the world to say, "*This is me*".

When we look out and into life through this collection of hypnotic thought, we are colouring the world that we perceive. Therefore, we perceive that which is not *real*, since thought usually interprets life based on what went beforehand (the past). Now, the past is nothing more than a memory trace, which when activated within our mind, obscures the present. Therefore a great deal of the *now* gets rejected if it is not in line with that which is stored in our memory – in our thoughts.

If we are experiencing life through thought contamination, then we perceive a delusion. This delusional mode of perception acts much like a fog, which obscures the purity that is our natural state, thereby disallowing us to perceive the natural Oneness of life as it truly is. Like peering out at life through a frosted window, we can never see clearly. Waking up from this is literally like waking up out of a dream, or shaking heavy smog from our mind. When we allow this to happen, we feel really good since it is a bit like emerging from a haze of fog, out into a clear sunny day with blue sky and not a cloud around.

So now, taking all of that into consideration; how have you and your world been thus far? Are you at peace? Are you happy or stressed, contented or miserable? What are you looking at life through? Do you see what you *think*, or do you see *what really is*? Are you keeping all of your favourite grievances in mind? Do you persistently relate your victim stories to others? Do you get upset when someone questions your belief system? Are you always reminding yourself and others of the people you have branded as being your enemies? What movie have you got playing in your mind; a fun loving comedy or a paranoid horror movie?

Can you dredge up the courage to look within your own mind, and identify what thoughts you are holding there? Can you be brave enough to see the links between your current experience of life, and the thoughts which are giving you that experience? For example, if you are not at peace, then realize that it is only because you are viewing life through this fog of thought. Peace occurs within a mind which *chooses* to be at peace within itself. The only thing in this whole wide world which has the power to disturb your natural peace of mind is your thoughts. We may blame everyone else for our lack of peace. We may blame our job or our life circumstances, but a fact which cannot be disputed, even by the most ardent of victim mentalities, is that the thoughts which we hold do indeed contaminate our natural state of peace.

Now, the quickest way to clean up our awareness is to allow an awakening to occur within us. Since the spiritual Oneness of life is the only Truth there really is, why would we not allow the Truth to be born again within our awareness? It feels a hell of a lot better to live from Truth, rather than to live life whilst gazing at a mental movie. In order for you to come to realization of the One, you simply have to allow your awareness to clear of what you currently have it filled with. Just like any old habit in life; when we break the habit, it usually doesn't arise much in our awareness anymore. But, I guess it all depends upon what we really want.

So, now can be your 'crunch' time if you so desire it to be. Are you finally ready for now? Half-hearted approaches don't work. When we have made our decision definite, then awakening becomes easy. It's like a person on a diet, or like someone who wants to quit smoking. The driving force behind their success is their absolute burning *desire* for the result they hope to attain. So now, what do you *really* desire?

4

Hypnotic Thought Dramas

The unreality of thought:

About twenty five years ago, here in my own home town in Ireland, a visiting stage hypnotist called a man up onto the stage and performed a rather funny trick. He hypnotized the man into believing that he no longer had a belly button. When the man in question checked his belly button, he freaked out, as he couldn't actually see his belly button there at all. He then ran at the hypnotist, grabbing him by the collar, demanding that he give him back his belly button. This man was so frantic that he even rushed off the stage and began accusing various members of the audience of stealing his belly button. As the story goes, the poor guy didn't realize that his belly button was there all along until the following morning.

We hear many stories like this about hypnotists throughout the world. Some are fake and others are true. It's amazing though, is it not, that somehow a hypnotist can plant a stupid thought like, *"someone stole your belly button"* into the mind of a man, and that man believes it so much, that he can't even see the belly button when he looks for it? I guess this is something like what happens to people who suffer from anorexia, for example, they see an overweight person when they look in the mirror, yet the reality is something entirely different.

Are any of us really that much different from the man who lost his belly button? Consider what kind of thoughts we believe about ourselves that are simply not an actual reality.

What kind of thoughts are we running in our minds every day? How is it that one day we feel great and the next day we are in a bad mood? External circumstances make us that way, you may say, but I would suggest that we should maybe look a little closer to home. Look into your mind and see the thoughts which you hold about yourself and your life. Do you believe those thoughts to be absolutely true, just like the man who lost his belly button did? Are you weaving a happy hypnosis of thought in your mind, or are you casting a dark hypnotic spell of poor me? Both are untrue you know, they are only thoughts, not reality. Reality lies outside of the hypnotic spell of thought, untouched by it.

Paranoia, phobias and depression etc, all have particular thought patterns to them. We have to think a thought and then believe that thought to be reality, before we experience an outcome of paranoia, phobia or depression. Do depressed people fill their minds with happy thoughts? As you think, so shall it be!

So, in order for a hypnotist to be successful, he needs to plant a thought in someone's mind and then get them to unquestioningly believe that the thought is reality. We do this within our own minds every day. We go about thinking our thoughts to be true all the time. Look at religion for another example. We are hypnotized with the beliefs of a particular religion. We have absolutely no proof that what the religions say is true, yet because we have had it all drummed into us, possibly from birth, we unquestioningly believe it anyway, and we get rather angry when others question our religious beliefs. Nowadays, we have people ready to blow themselves up in suicide attacks, in order to defend their religious beliefs. How more hypnotized could one get?

People are running to therapy more so now than ever before. Depression is also a growing problem. What kind of thoughts are we holding in our minds to produce these effects? These thoughts have a hypnotic effect upon our awareness, they then affect the health of our bodies through the stress they create, and unless we become alert to the thought dramas we are holding, is there any chance we will shake them off at all?

Yet although life can get tough at times, our minds make it even tougher, just by focusing on the negative aspects of it. Even happy people have their dire moments to deal with, yet possibly someone who is generally happy won't dwell on the negative aspects of life so much.

Phobias (of spiders, socialising and flying etc) and beliefs we may hold in us 'having' an inferiority complex are good examples of hypnosis also. None of these phobias or complexes are true, but we believe they are and therefore they are reflected into our reality. Sometimes, a particular thought or set of thoughts can leave us paralyzed with unrealistic fear, over some trivial thing like a small spider.

We are indeed hypnotized with our self-image. That sense of 'me' was put in place through years of thought conditioning, from our parents, brothers and sisters, teachers, television, friends, peer groups and also ourselves. When we become an adult, we think that we can give an honest appraisal of who we are to others, based upon our deeply conditioned and hypnotized self-image (thought identity).

We make the declaration, *"I am Jack the banker"*, yet banking is not what we are, but simply something that we do. We say, *"I am afraid of flying"*, yet fear of flying is a thought which we have come to believe is real through our repetition of that belief in our mind. It's hypnotized into our awareness; in the same way the guy believed he had no belly button. None of it has any actual reality outside of thought.

I remember before I got involved in studying spirituality and the mind, I held a phobia (set of thoughts I believed without question) which led to me fearing social settings. Sometimes I would deliberately not go out in social settings, because I believed that it was a fearful thing to do. I recall the thoughts which used to pop into my mind when a new person would speak to me - *they don't notice me - I can't hold a conversation – I'm a quiet person.* I remember how my chest would tighten

47

as I tried to fight these thoughts. Usually I would just leave whatever party I was at earlier than I had planned to and go home.

This hypnosis was not real, yet I believed these thoughts to be true, much in the same way as the guy who believed he had no belly button. As a result, those thoughts affected my reality and I unconsciously ended up creating that unreality within myself. The result was that I wouldn't speak when I was in a crowd with people. Even if I had something worthwhile to add to a conversation (which I usually had), I would not say it out loud, because I believed (I was hypnotized) that I was a quiet person.

My awareness was saturated with a dream constructed unreality, with my everyday thoughts as the author of that unreality. Whilst I was in that hypnotic spell, I never questioned the strange thoughts that held me captive, just as one never questions the reality of a nightmare whilst one is lost in it. We only know that the nightmare is not real when we awaken from it. However, when I got involved in spirituality, it talked a lot about awakening from the nightmare of a thought induced unreality. I learned about how we are all conditioned (hypnotized), and how easily we believed to be true each thought that passed through our awareness.

This was a revelation for me, so I gathered as much spiritual knowledge as I could get my hands on. This was so I could figure out how to experience first-hand the Reality of the One, which I was learning all about. Little did I know, that the One was staring me in the face all along, and all of the head knowledge in the world, was of no use when it came to simply switching my attention from thought to Reality. I came to grasp, that I didn't really need a whole lot of spiritual head knowledge, in order to see that the hypnotic spell called 'me' was a smokescreen to eclipse my awareness of Reality. I could then see that, in fact, too much spiritual head knowledge was a part of the trap, used by the ego to imprison us in concepts, philosophy and beliefs, rather than to simply allow an authentic awakening to take place.

Spiritual knowledge:

A lot of seekers add spiritual knowledge and experience onto their ego. This operates like an update upon the old withered out and dried up defunct ego, which possibly wasn't doing a very good job until spirituality arrived on the scene. When the ego gets its teeth into the spiritual scene, then spiritual knowledge and experience may temporarily alleviate any inferiority complex which may be held within that ego. All too often I have witnessed this alleviating effect, take on the characteristics that are the reverse of the inferiority complex. The ego then adopts the superiority complex for itself.

This leaves the 'new' updated and knowledgeable ego with a persona (mask) of specialness and holier than thou-ness. We may find a belief growing within us, that we are holier or more spiritual than other people; that everyone else is a miserable sinner, and we are better than they are. Some spiritual minded people often feel that they have the answer to all of the world's ills, and they may make it their duty to save the poor miserable 'sinners' of the world. Now, saving the world usually entails you (the 'saved' recipient) accepting whatever spiritual beliefs are being held by the one doing the saving. As a result, you will be hypnotized by someone else's concepts or spiritual beliefs. This 'save the world' belief shows an underlying attitude of superiority. Perhaps you will disagree, but don't a lot of spiritual institutions claim to be the main guys who know 'God' better than the rest?

I found this to be the case from my own personal experience upon the spiritual seeking scene. For over ten years I did everything I assumed a Truth seeker should be doing. So for a long time, I felt like I had all of the answers. Everyone else was living a normal kind of life, whereas I had my life devoted to spirituality. This gave me the false idea that I was in some way better or more 'spiritual' than others. I accumulated a vast amount of book knowledge, which of course meant that I took great pride in reciting it to others. The accumulation of spiritual knowledge left me with an attitude of spiritual grandiosity. I was not aware enough of this hypnotic drama within my thought system, until it weighed down heavily upon me. As a result, my spiritual stereotype image came crumbling down, and I felt like my life was turning into a hell of sorts.

After the constant and unending acquirement of spiritual knowledge, it seemed to me that it was all just a waste of time and effort. The knowledge wasn't producing any fruit within me. I noticed how my thoughts loved to pour over the spiritual knowledge all the time. Inside my head, I would have thought dramas based around spirituality running 24-7. The voice in my head would be constantly philosophizing, debating and trying to figure out the Truth of Reality with thought, rather than through direct experience.

However, when this house of knowledge came crumbling down all around me, I found life beginning to get meaningless again. Even the hypnotic thought drama of spiritual knowledge, does not satisfy our minds need for entertainment and distraction forever. Whenever we reach a point, when deep within all we truly want is freedom, we tend to leave the clever and knowledgeable thought dramas behind. It is then that we start to walk the walk, rather than talk the talk.

When we get to this point, when we cannot find enough 'spiritual' food for thought to chew upon, we get to the state of boredom. The thoughts in our mind are bored because we can't find anything to stimulate them; we don't have enough interesting little dramas going on, to get our mind chewing upon. If we go deeper with this boredom, where the thought entity has been there, done that, worn the same old t-shirt, and we find ourselves fed up with the same old rig-marole, then we could even end up with a mild depression coming upon us. This is where I finally arrived, after my ten years of spiritual investigation.

Leaving behind thought dramas:

When we lose our sense of meaning in life, we may use escape mechanisms like alcohol or drugs, in order to get out of our pain of no meaning. These escapist substances may temporarily relieve the pain associated with a thought induced un-reality, because they take us out of our heads so to speak, or better put, out of our thought dramas. They temporarily relieve the hypnosis we are under, and then we don't feel so caught up inside our thoughts. Is it any wonder that people who abuse these substances refer to intoxication as getting out of their heads? We paint pictures and all kinds of crazy scenarios inside our heads, all day long. Then we actually wonder to ourselves, why we are not at peace.

I wasted a lot of my seeking years weaving a dream within my awareness of 'me' the stereotype 'Truth' seeker, rather than taking a good honest look at the content of thought which was hypnotizing me. When I did look into my mind, I observed a landscape of horror movies. I uncovered all kinds of madness, which I feel everyone has in their mind, but we all just take it as being normal. Perhaps most of us, don't even know that this hypnosis is there at all. The voice in my head (the commentator) was hypnotizing me every day with random thought scenarios, which would then escalate into full scale dramas (mental movies).

It horrified me to observe how hypnotized I was with these on-going dramas. I tolerated them throughout my spiritual search, because they were obviously leaning more toward a happy hypnotic spell then, rather than the misery go round they transformed back into. Formal meditation was supposed to clear one's mind of this type of trash, yet here this trash was still inside my head, and not only that, I was totally and unknowingly mesmerized by it all. I began to feel like I had wasted many years seeking, only to have it all amounting to nothing. So, I figured the only way to shake this hypnosis off, was to get an understanding of what it was I was really dealing with. So let me go a little deeper with the precursor of experience I had, before Reality dawned upon me.

I closed my eyes and paid attention within my mind, watching the random thoughts coming and going, weaving their dreams. I never made any attempt to stop them or direct them in any way, like what I spent years doing in meditation. I just observed the thoughts and nothing more. I noticed something peculiar happening. I began to understand that my attention was sleeping, and this then allowed the thought dramas to create the hypnotic effect upon my awareness all day long. My awareness was then saturated in daydreams. However, I realized that the very act of observing in the present helped to clear my awareness of those thoughts, because I was awakening my attention out of dreamland, just by observing.

When I shifted my attention to observing, I noticed that thought was no longer saturating my awareness. It reminded me of taking a pot of water off the boil. When we lift a pot off the boil the bubbles stop rising in the pot. This is what I noticed happening in my mind; thoughts simmered down whilst I was observing with Attentive Presence. It became clear to me that by merely paying attention to life as it is, the hypnotic spell was broken.

I then understood experientially, that the thoughts which I always called 'me' were not actually me at all. I could use my attention as an observer, which I realized is the mode needed to be aware of Reality. Or I could have my attention sleeping in thought dramas, which would then hypnotize my awareness with daydream scenarios, and that false sense of a separate 'me'. Then it clicked with me, that the *being present* which the gurus were talking about, was another way of saying _pay attention_. So obviously, I finally understood that Attentive Presence is what clears the awareness of hypnotic thought, due to the attention being awakened from the thought dream.

I grasped that Attentive Presence is the foundation upon which perception of the One stands. This Reality clearly cannot be perceived, by a mind that has its attention sleeping in a daydream. Nor can it be perceived by a mind which maintains a fixed viewpoint that the outer world has to change first, before the inner world can come to a state of peace.

When we realize that a chaotic outer situation will not be solved with a chaotic mind; then possibly we will allow our mind to be at peace, for only a peaceful mind can see clearly how to *really* solve outer problems. In most cases, a peaceful mind will see that many of these so called 'problems' which we focus upon, are merely mental phantoms (our mind playing tricks on us) and can simply be dismissed as being trivial non-issues. However, an awakened mind will also be able to take positive action to solve 'real' outer problems - without the mental turmoil. Whereas, a mind filled with thought dramas, will only ever create more unnecessary dramas.

Now, the awakening of attention to the One takes no time at all, only a true willingness to let these thought dramas go. Even though our awareness may be totally saturated with hypnotic thought dramas, any of us could begin today by shifting into Attentive Presence. I have found from my own experience that the old habit-momentum of daydreaming slows down as each day passes, but only when we are determined to stay out of thought dramas and allow awakening instead.

We can so easily drift back into a daydream state, if we are not truly willing to keep the thought trash out of our mind. This attentive mode of observation helps to keep our wits about us. When we have our wits about us, we are very sharp mentally, so if any thought trash comes our way, we are alert to it immediately. Then we have the choice of whether or not we wish to get tied up in the trash or ignore it. If we get tied up in it, then once again our awareness will be saturated in thought dramas and unreality. If we ignore the trash and stick with Attentive Presence, then the Spirit and perception of Oneness will grow stronger in our awareness. Over each day that we keep our minds free from the hypnotic spell of thought, we will become more deeply aware of Truth and Reality.

Now, I was finally willing to admit that the change needed to occur within me and not in the world outside. I understood that the voice in my head (the commentator) had to go. I was so fed up with the misery go round of thought interference in my life, that now; when I finally understood where the problem was really coming from, I naturally turned my back on the commentator inside my head. However, I could still hear the commentator ranting for a while, pleading to have its old job back of ruining my life. But easily my attention would switch from thought to Reality more and more, until making that switch of attention became a habit, like any other habit.

Thought creates a dreamlike world of appearance and deception, a charade we all mistake for Reality, when it sure as hell is anything but Reality. I yearned for the Truth to grow within me, tall and strong. I needed this Reality more than I needed anything else. I no longer wanted to be under a hypnotic spell; I wanted no thought to taint this purity which was beginning to grow within me.

As I let go of thought dramas, I became aware that the hard concrete world of the ego was brightening up with pristine clarity. The voice in my head, I noticed, was trying to interfere with its usual analytical conceptualization of how I was now feeling, but that was futile at this stage. I just wasn't interested in that analytical knowledge stuff anymore, or the dreams it produced in my mind. I no longer felt the need to tell people about this growth which was occurring within my awareness. I only wanted to savour it and be at ease with it all. I didn't want to interfere with this awakening. I only wanted to be at peace, within the embrace of Reality, Spirit or the One.

Now, will the mind made egoic 'me' rise again to sabotage our awareness of Truth? Well, when we reach that pinnacle of no interest in thought dramas (the head game), it is a bit like casting a smelly piece of rubbish into your bin. Do you go nose diving into your scrap heap to retrieve a piece of smelly rubbish? I think not, unless you really do love dreaming the hypnotic thought drama of hell. I gaze upon the old thought dramas that once hypnotized me as an unfortunate blip, of a bygone era when darkness stalked my mind and life. I have no interest in returning to the darkness, I now love the light of Reality far too much. I now stay firmly within that embrace of Reality, patrolling the perimeters of my mind every day, observing and keeping tight security against intrusion from that withered corpse of hypnotic thought.

So, what is your target? What do you want? Peace or drama, a dream or Reality? Only we can ask ourselves these questions, because nobody can tell us what our target should be, and nobody can force or compel us into waking up from the dream state either. Also, nobody can magically awaken us, because others can only give directions. However, what are we going to do with those directions?

Do we, as possible Truth seekers, actually want the ultimate Truth that sets one free from the onslaught of hypnotic thought? Or do we love our thought dramas far too much? We need to know the target we are aiming at, in order to actually have any chance of hitting it. Only we can decide what is right for us, only we can decide if what we want from spirituality will be realized in our lives. Only we have the power within ourselves, to finally put an end to the hypnotic delusion which we engage in every day.

Let's not waste our own time, because we are wasting our own valuable time, if we know that we don't truly want to step away from the dreams and back into Reality. Our current dream may be nice and pleasant, however if we prefer to sleep in dreams, then we are still slaves to thought, whether or not our dream is a nice one or a living hell. On the other hand, being in Reality, releases us into the ever abundant, peaceful and joyous flow of life now. Setting us free at last – free at last!

5

Liar Liar

A substitute for Reality:

Now, brace yourself, you may not like what I'm about to say. It has become clear to me that the world is filled to the throat with liars. Of course, I'm not referring to the average type of liar we are all familiar with, like politicians or gossips. The type of liar I'm referring to lives within the mind of everyone on Earth, quite unbeknownst to the majority of humanity of course. The inner liar, or commentator, has become something of a substitute for Reality and it also drowns out the voice of our Spirit, so to speak. Or better put; because we choose to listen to this little mad voice, we cannot hear the voice of our Spirit any longer. It practically leaves our intuition comatose, and the guidance we would receive from that intuition, no longer reach's our awareness. This leads us away from going with the flow of life, which is so intrinsic for awakening to have any lasting effect.

Folks are always telling themselves lies, as they reconstruct or alter within their mind the so called 'reality' they are faced with daily. We re-run the daily events within our mind, and we overwrite what has happened with what we think should've happened. We do this so life will appear to fall into line with whatever fantasy we think should be, instead of the Reality of what is. When we 'alter' reality in this mental manner, we tend to feel a little more certain that life is as we *think* it is, even if that perceived life is a nightmare.

Everywhere we go, we meet folks who want to tell us about their altered realities (daydreams) and not about Reality at all. We fill our minds with mental aberrations, delusions and fantasies of who we think we are, and we dream up scary epics of what might be. Then we react to these hallucinations within our mind as if they are real, but all the while we are telling ourselves lies.

I have to endure folk telling me lies all the time. They don't realize they are doing this of course, since as I said, they believe in the lies they are speaking. They tell me things like, *"I am this"* or *"I am that type of person"*, but they don't appear to realize that the 'I' which they are referring to is a construct of thought only. These thoughts of *"I am this"* or *"I am that type of person"* all arise from memories of experiences which have happened in the past. It is these memories which add the very convincing appearance (illusion) of separate selfhood to the mind. From memory we derive our entire sense of 'me'. We remember who we *think* we are, based on what went beforehand. In other words, we <u>remember</u> our entire sense of identity into existence. So, if we lost our memory, well then, who would we be?

Now, memory is nothing but thought, therefore our whole sense of 'me' is equal to thought and thought only. The commentator (voice of the ego) takes this thought and turns it into stories, which it then tells to itself and also to the world at large. The stories all relate to a 'me' and we become the hero or the victim of our story. But we should realize that this is all a dream. We are not our past, or the stories we spin in our heads. We are not heroes or victims; we are pure life energy (the One) masquerading as myriads of separate somebody's who have stories to tell.

This sense of separation leaves us feeling cut off from the Oneness of life, and we feel isolated or alone within the great pantomime called 'my life'. The story keeps the psychological construct of 'me' intact until we are willing to see beyond the thought dramas which hold it in place. The commentator is hypnotizing us with its constant internal gibber jabber, with its mental movies and its thought scenarios. That is why people are always telling themselves lies, unknowingly of course. These lies have become the substitute for Reality.

Now, hopefully this should become clearer to you as we go along, because if it does resonate with you, then maybe you will finally be able to _see through_ the little charade your ego has set in place, which distorts your true identity and spiritual awareness.

The psychological 'me' or ego:

Most of us mechanically react to every thought which passes through our awareness, as if it were based upon absolute Reality. These thoughts form a pattern in our mind, which then becomes somewhat dreamlike. These dreams tend to saturate our awareness, forming a tapestry weaved of delusional beliefs, psychological fears and phobias, paranoia's, neurosis, inferiorities, superiorities and complexes. These dreams combine, taking a place in our memory, and then they form the hypnotized character I refer to as the ego.

The ego is a lie of course, it is made of thought programmes or dreams which we have become hypnotized with. These dreams are all unknowing lies; we know not what we do, so to speak. And as long as we allow the commentator to hypnotize us on a daily basis with its daydreams and internal commentary, we never will fully know what we do. Nor will we ever really know our true spiritual nature, due to the commentator taking a place in our awareness where the Spirit should be.

Before I awakened from the sleep of hypnotic thought, I couldn't recognize the lies which I told myself. I clung to beliefs and philosophies in the same manner as many today cling to new age or non-dual philosophy. I clung to these beliefs and philosophies mainly for the comfort and sense of certainty they

58

appeared to give me. Anyone who called these mental distortions into question got frowned upon. I built a fortress around my beliefs, simply because they made the world appear more stable, and therefore less chaotic. My beliefs gave me seeming assurances that I knew all about life, death, the meaning of existence and what lay in the 'afterlife'. I was completely wrong of course, since all of this was nothing more than hypnotic thought programming in action. It was a spell of thought I had set in place, to make my life appear more stable.

Then, when I allowed my awareness to clear of the thought dramas (lies) I tended to believe in, it became quite startling to observe the lies which others believed about themselves and their lives. It was only then that I realized the extent to which most people have their entire sense of selfhood, derived from hypnotic thought programming (lies).

The source of these thought programmes are obviously built up over the course of a lifetime. But when we truly desire to step outside of this trash and see beyond it all, then these programmes are relinquished fairly easily. Once relinquished or better put - *seen through*, the One comes to the forefront of our awareness, and we then begin to perceive the natural Oneness of all life. Indeed, when we do finally relinquish thought dramas, it can be almost funny when you come to recall the trash you once had your mind filled with. You may find yourself shaking your head in disbelief, when you recognize how hypnotized you have been.

Hypochondriacs are good examples of thought programming. Hypochondriacs have their sense of 'me' derived from imagining that they are sick all the time. They will feed this belief heavily because that is who they think they are - *'Me' the sick person*. In most cases their sickness is not real, but merely thoughts playing a game inside their mind. But most hypochondriacs are attracted to the game thought plays with them; it's familiar to them, and this familiarity strengthens the seeming stability of the psychological 'me'. So therefore, we should not assume that they would want to be 'cured' of their mental malignancy any time soon. If their sense of personhood ('me') comes from being 'the one who is always sick', then if you take that away from them, you would be more or less taking away a large chunk of their thought made identity (ego).

It's the same with some people who seem hell bent on holding onto phobias and the likes. The ego doesn't think that life will be as stable or familiar if it gets relinquished, and when life isn't seen as being stable and familiar, it can be misperceived that life is quite frightening. Exposing the unreality of the psychological 'me' is a scary thing to be doing to a hypochondriac, or indeed, it can be a very frightening thing to a lot of people, who might also obtain a sense of stability from their thought constructed psychological 'me'. This also includes many Truth seekers, who have their whole sense of 'me' wrapped up in being 'me' the 'spiritual' person.

I recall hearing one of my local doctors complain once, that almost 85% of his time was taken up with hypochondriacs. He said that he was seriously considering giving up the whole doctor thing, because he was so sick of them. No matter how often he told them that there was nothing wrong with them, they would argue that there was something wrong. Some of these hypochondriacs would even fall out with him, and then go visiting *another* doctor until they got the 'verdict' they desired – until someone else agreed with the lies they believed in about who they are. It is important to the hypochondriac that others view them in the way they see themselves, because if it was proven that they are not what they think they are, then what are they? They would feel completely lost without that seemingly 'stable' sense of 'me'.

Perhaps you know of someone who likes to tell you fairy stories about their life, or about who they like to think they are. Maybe they are not a hypochondriac but something similar, like a paranoid person who believes that the world is conspiring against them, or someone who thinks they are 'king of the hill' or maybe just someone who believes that they have a phobia. You should try telling them that what they believe isn't true at all, but is just a few thoughts rattling around inside their mind which they have hypnotized themselves with. And then prepare to take your guard, as you behold the irritation growing within them right before your eyes.

It can be quite shocking, seeing some of the reactions you will get from pointing out the truth. You see, you will be messing with their *altered* reality and pulling at their sense of 'me'. If there is one thing I have come to understand the hard way, it's this simple fact - folks don't like having their altered realities or thought made psychological 'me' messed with, at least not until it causes their life to become extremely boring, or until it turns their life into a living hell.

Fear of the One:

After awakening, I could then see clearly that the majority of humanity (some more so than others), really believed the stories they filled their minds with. It became quite clear to me, that the egos whole sense of 'me' was nothing more than a delusion to replace our true identity as Spirit. When I was a seeker, I read all about the ego being a delusion, but I never really understood it until I let go of my own delusions.

These stories we fill our minds with tend to maintain an illusion of control. If our view of life and the world seems predictable and controllable, then life doesn't seem to be such a scary business, does it? Well, when we think we know what is going to happen tomorrow-week or tomorrow-month, well then, that's manageable isn't it? We then *think* we have life by the short and curly's. We dream that we are in the driving seat, firmly with our hands upon the steering wheel of life's flowing current don't we?

Then again, maybe we tell ourselves stories just to relieve some of the boredom we might be feeling. Indeed, anything will do as long as it fills up the emptiness, as long as it fills up the Void nature of the One. Unconsciously, we know this Void is there, and because we fear that it is a vacuum of nothingness, we do all that we can to avoid it, including telling ourselves depressing or scary stories.

Yes, we will try to 'become' anything in order to avoid the emptiness we fear might be our true nature. We will even try to become Truth seekers in order to avoid it, as we set about trying to create a new psychological spiritual 'me'. But in doing this, we are trying to strike a bargain with the Spirit, so we can hold onto our delusions and only pay lip service to the Truth, by turning it all into another philosophy. Our fear of what we think is Void and empty is the reason why the *true* truth speakers have always been burned at the stake, crucified, slandered and abused. It is perceived that the true Truth speakers are a danger and a threat to all that is 'me', even for the spiritual version of 'me' which many weave for themselves these days.

Yes, the ego will stamp out the Truth with its falsifications at all times, to keep at bay what it perceives as being emptiness, or the Void like nature of the One. These falsifications will usually emanate from teachers of the common and accepted ways. Now, the common way used to be organized religion, but is now the way of eastern methods. Seekers think they are being rather modern by leaving behind organized religion and taking up some eastern practice, but all that usually happens is that they swap one belief system for another.

It's the same with many who allow their awareness to be saturated in an apparent 'non-dual' philosophy. In fact, non-dual philosophy is fast becoming a new religion these days, and that's the worst thing that can ever happen to the teachings of awakening. Once those teachings are formalized, then it won't be long before they are institutionalized also. To my mind, this seems like an ego attempt of striking a compromise with the Spirit like, *"Let's settle for a new type of religion or a philosophy, instead of awakening."* Yet all this philosophy and organized effort, only ever serves to stand in the way of the Truth. The totality of life cannot be stuffed into the tiny boxes of our philosophies and religions. Reality transcends all of our tiny ideas and belief systems. Reality truly is Void or empty of such thought contamination.

We fear that the One is a vacant emptiness. There is a mental image which comes from ego that the realization of Spirit involves a blank state, where we will be in a kind of weird empty trance, with a nothingness of all sensation. We fear that we will be left with a dry and arid mode of being. This is what the ego would have us believe anyway. But you have to understand that the opposite is the case. This Void or the One cannot strictly be called emptiness; it is actually pure fullness. It is the pinnacle of all life, the climax which humanity and all life forms strive for. It is that which gives life to all that we perceive, and all that we are. The animals are that, the ocean is that, the air is that, the Earth is that, your greatest enemy is that and so also is your best friend that. This Void is *you*. This is our absolute Truth.

But we still fear our spiritual Truth, and we prefer to spin stories within our mind as a replacement for our true being. The stories could relate to anything at all, as long as it is *not* the Truth. This is when the ego comes in handy. The ego, being nothing more than a collection of thought, will always try to take the place of our true identity as the One.

Altering reality:

At the very moment you open your eyes in the morning, you construct within your mind all of what you think you are, and all of how you perceive the world to be. Maybe you *remind* yourself that you are a stressed person, or that the world is a terrible place. Maybe you bring to mind that you are an unhappy or neurotic person. Maybe you tell yourself that life is tough; *"It's a rat race out there, it's kill or be killed"*. The possible combinations for lies are endless.

Lie upon lie, you construct an altered reality within your mind. You look out and into life through this make believe thought world, and all you ever see is your lies. Your make believe is spread out over the world, tainting everything you come upon, from your own self-image, to your perception of others, to the world as you perceive it to be. Now, what would it be like if you just woke up one morning, and allowed your mind to remain clear? What if you didn't bother to re-run all of those little _reminders_ of what you are, what others are and what the world is like? Yes, I wonder what life would be like then, huh?

You think you know who and what you are. You tell yourself your story of 'me' every day, and then you go out to meet the world, so you can tell everyone else you meet all the stories of 'me'. As you tell the stories of your 'great' adventures, of what you did and what you said, piece by little piece you attempt to convince the world and yourself, that you are what you _think_ you are. If enough of the world agrees that you are the semblance of this story called 'you', then it is copper fastened, isn't it? Well at least it is within _your_ mind anyway.

Here in your little dream of 'me' where the storyline hardly ever changes, you try to maintain a tightly held grip upon yourself and your life. You try to steer the wheel of your life, in accordance with all of what you think you are. You keep telling yourself that you are the great one, the inferior one, the neurotic or the hero. You label yourself as being a dentist, a doctor, a window cleaner or a shop keeper. All of this stuff hypnotizes your awareness with lies and with a thought made character which turns you into a puppet, which is being dangled by the strings of thought, and it is this state of affairs which we have come to call the 'waking' state.

Now, do you really want to wake up from the _familiarity_ of the dreams you are spinning within your mind? We may enjoy our lies, but we will never make them true, not even to ourselves, because there might come a day when the lies just won't do it for us anymore. Life has a way of crushing the fantasies of dreamers, so the Spirit can be allowed to take hold of the reigns. You may tolerate the struggle of grasping the reigns of life's chariot, of turbulently fighting against life's flow, but the stress of it all will eventually show up, and if you don't

64

surrender to the flow of Spirit, then that stress will wear you down, until maybe there is a breaking point. Hence, this is why people have nervous breakdowns, depressions and panic attacks; it's why they get run down with stress disorders and the likes.

So now, how much do you really want to stand face to face, with the unadorned Truth of your Reality? You know, there will be no *lasting* realization of Truth, until we are willing to see through all of our lies. We may have momentary glimpses of Truth, but awakening to Reality is not about momentary glimpses, it is about an abiding realization. That is not to say that it is like some unending buzz, like you have popped an illegal pill and are then permanently high, mystically charged with super powers. It is merely about recognizing the lies as lies, and choosing Reality instead. *The lies are just thoughts*, so in any moment of time we have the choice of either joining our attention with thought or Reality. By making this choice, we will easily see through all of the lies we have been cherishing.

Is it easy to see through the lies? Yes it is; but how do you see through the lies? Well, you've got to realize that the voice in your mind is telling you lies to begin with, and then you have to be brave enough to admit that fact to yourself. Now, which do you see yourself as? Do you see yourself as being one who wants the Truth, or as the one who wishes to be a sleepwalker? Can you stomach the truth? As some poor lost soul once said to me, *"Look, I know it's the truth, but I just don't want to hear about it"*.

Yes, all of those little hang-ups, the inferiorities and superiorities; all of those little inner lies (thoughts) have to be seen for the *mirage* which they are if you want Reality to take hold. But who would you be without all of that trash cluttering up your mind? Yes indeed, who would you be? I can tell you for sure, that who you would be, is what you *really* are. You would be trading your limited thought identity (ego), for realization of your inner abundant Truth and Reality. That Truth and Reality being the One undivided and Omni-present source of all.

6

Where the flow don't go, I don't go!

All the world's a stage:

The Truth - now what is difficult about that? Surely there is no effort required in being true? Obviously effort is required only in being false. Effort is needed to maintain an illusion of what we like to think we are. Effort is required when we are pretending, or when we are acting the part of something we are not. Effort is needed to uphold the false face of ego which we try to project upon the world.

When we live our lives from ego, we may feel that it is important for the world to view us in a particular manner. We all want to be liked, loved and accepted by our friends, family and society. So we might feel it necessary, to alter our personality to fit in with the world around us. We might carry around two faces, or maybe three or four faces, depending on whomever it is we are speaking with. This is tantamount to an act we put on for the world; it's like we are actors and the world is our stage. Most of us are putting on the very same act. It's almost as if we are seeking for applause from the world around us, or for the world to tell us, *"Heh, now that you have conformed, we accept you"*.

Maybe applause *is* what we are seeking, so we can counteract the inferior thoughts and knock-on feelings of unworthiness we use to dress ourselves in daily. Could these

66

thoughts and feelings of unworthiness, be the reason why we are always caught in the effort of trying to become this or that? Could they be the reason why we are always trying to 'become' anything or anyone at all, just as long as it is not what we actually are? Why are we always trying to run away from ourselves, by tampering with our natural born character? Why do we throw away that naturally occurring uniqueness of character, which the Spirit appears willing to uphold?   Will there ever come a time, when we will all learn to accept ourselves for what we really are?

Many go to great lengths to fit in with what they perceive as being 'others'. But these supposed 'others' are most likely clones of society, more or less. They are also actors, treating you like you are *their* audience. Really and truly, in Reality, they actually are the same source-energy that you are. They are One with you. Strictly speaking, they are you, and you are they.

So stop reading now, and give someone a pat on the back for being a great actor. Tell them that they are maintaining a great act; a grand illusion. It's so grand in fact, that the people of the world are totally spellbound by it all. They don't even realize they are acting. They think they *are* what their mind tells them they are. Many will even fool themselves into believing that the role they are playing is *real*. It can almost get to a point where we play our role so well, that we no longer know with any certainty what our true natural character is like. This is when the mind gets disorientated, and begins to confuse Reality with dreamland.

However, as we try to create a mask of thought identity (ego) which has embedded in it all of the qualities which we think society will accept, what we are actually doing is creating lots of mental effort, which interferes with our naturally occurring character.   We are filling ourselves with fear unbeknownst to ourselves, with the mantra, *"what if they don't like me?"* However, tampering with that pure spiritual nature and natural character gives rise to an illusion, and that is what we meet when we speak to most people in any given day - an illusion!

All folk like to think of themselves in a particular way. We think of ourselves as being a certain type of person, with certain fears, neurosis, complexes and inadequacies etc. We will even go to great effort, exhausting our life energy into 'keeping up appearances' for the friends who we treat like an audience. But all of that thought stuff is not what we are. We are that Reality which lies beyond, and gives power to, all of the thought stuff in our mind.

Everyone knows how children often imitate people they are surrounded by on a daily basis. This imitation becomes a habit, and soon we find that we have adopted the tastes, beliefs, ways and mannerisms of others, and we then make those tastes, beliefs, ways and mannerisms part and parcel of our thought made identity (ego). This ego then overwrites our naturally occurring character, and also all of the inborn traits which gives us a sense of uniqueness. We might then grow up feeling like we are being suffocated by the world around us, as we try to conform to what we think we should be. This gives rise to stress, depression or a sense of being unfulfilled, simply because we are not living our life in the way we were naturally wired to live it.

The ego is an imposter, which is trying to take the place of our natural character; it is trying to drown out the voice of our Spirit and the guidance we would naturally receive from that Spirit. The inner spiritual guidance enlivens us to action, whenever we go with the flow of life, living our lives for the moment. However, the ego is like a form of hypnosis and we are instead hypnotized with thoughts and beliefs, which we now call 'me'. Therefore this has made what we now call our 'personality' very much like a second hand identity.

Yet all the while, the Spirit is trying to live in accordance with the natural characteristics we were born into this world with. But we keep stifling, pushing down and ignoring the call of the Spirit and our natural character. We instead listen to what the world has to say about who we should be, or what we should 'become'. So we try to alter our natural self by trying to 'become' what everyone else thinks we should 'become'. We ignore our natural characters talents and passions, and instead we dance to the repetitive and boring beat of society and its clone like monotony of endless becoming.

Now, is that what we really are? Are we no more than a mixture of other people and our cultures learning's, living through us in a mechanical and hypnotic manner? Of course, ego shifts and changes to various degrees from year to year. So can something which shifts and changes so much, really be said to be something that is of a true and lasting quality? It's like the weather; one day it's cold and rainy, and the next day it's hot and sunny. So if the weather could talk and claim to have a sense of 'me', what could it possibly say about itself? The impermanence of the rain and sun coming and going, cannot be said to be the true identity of the weather. So it could not say, "*I am hot, cold, rainy or sunny*". The only response or description it could possibly give of itself, from the perspective of its true and lasting quality, would be to simply say, "*I Am*".

To say 'I Am' is the only thing which cannot be disputed. Everything else will come and go, but that sense of 'I Am' never wavers. It is always there, and it is the only thing which will *ever* be true or real. Ego is an attempt to add onto the sense of 'I Am'. Ego says "*I am this*" or "*I am that*", which is a false perception of the self. However, to find the Real we have to bypass ego, and with our awareness clear we need to embrace our natural characteristics. This leaves us awakened to our true natural state, and then life no longer feels like such an up-hill struggle.

Many of the rules of religion or of the new age movement, also lead us to fight against our natural character, as we try to 'become' what we think is 'spiritual'. This only leaves us digging our way deeper into the thought world. Now, the awakened are only interested in stepping outside of the thought world, and *all* of its thought made models, which aim at stuffing

Spirit and the One into the tiny boxes of our thought made systems of belief and philosophy. The awakened recognize that both belief and philosophy tend to distort the simplicity of awakening, leading those who seek for awakening to talk and think more about it all, rather than to actually awaken in the here and now. It leads them to fight against their natural self, as they try to become or to conform to the dictates laid down by these various systems of _thought_.

The awakened mainly ignore or overlook the egos spiritual thought world, its thought dramas and its belief systems. They realize that it is all like a mirage, which you can gaze upon and be fooled by if you were momentarily unawares, but there is no way that you will be fully sucked into thinking that it is all real. No belief has any truth to it, because belief is mere thought. Spirit holds the only Truth there is, and this fact is not a belief but a living Reality!

And so, the world has many religions and philosophies which do not serve the Truth at all, but merely serve the interests of the guys who pitch those stories to the world. This all keeps the drama and the wheel of becoming spinning never-endingly. It keeps us all forever chasing after our true spiritual nature. Yet, when we do finally allow ourselves to step outside of the delusions in order to find our Reality, we will see clearly that these systems only attempt to keep us busy with the endless 'becoming' of something that we are not, whilst pushing out of our awareness the _All_ that we are.

Letting the steering wheel go:

All of our hankering after happiness and seeking for connection with 'others', is merely a reflection of that innate desire to awaken to our true state of Oneness. But we do not trust that the Spirit will make our everyday lives lighter, peaceful and more care free. So we cling desperately to the steering wheel of our lives, not giving the Spirit a chance to brighten things up for us. Due to our lack of trust in that Spirit, we feel that we can plan for our peace and happiness even better than the Spirit can. We think we can imitate unity or Oneness with our egoic substitutions.

For awakening and true Oneness to survive within you it requires trust, for you are literally handing over control of your life to your inner higher power. I say 'higher' because this power is of the Spirit, which knows how to live better than your ego does. The ego usually hasn't got a clue whether it is coming or going, hence the reason why ego and that sense of being unfulfilled usually go hand in hand. Through awakening you will be letting go of the defective control stick you have been turbulently running your life with. You are that higher power. That higher power is within you as your true nature, so really you are handing over control of your life to your true Self. The ego is not your true Self; it is an alteration we make, or a substitution for our true nature. It requires effort and energy to maintain because it is literally not *true*, therefore it also requires control.

Usually we have a tight grip upon our lives, trying to control every aspect of it. As we attempt to plan for the future we usually get tense, stressed and fearful due to our being afraid that we will screw it all up. So therefore, with awakening to survive within us, we need to give up this control and _trust_ that our inner Truth can do a better job. All of those personality defects which we are constantly fighting against or trying to subdue, are no longer a problem whenever we live from Spirit. Spirit, in Reality is unstained by the blemishes of the thought entity, and this Truth becomes quite obvious as we allow awakening to occur.

But instead of trusting and flowing with the Spirit; as another alternative, many spiritual minded people will instead often hanker after ways to control or to make their lives work. They are always digging into their past and seeking methods to heal that illusive 'inner child'. They struggle to do all kinds of work – body work, energy work, mind training and working out karma etc. Listening to them, would make one feel that life is really supposed to be a joyless chore, instead of the great adventure it was meant to be.

I know this from experience, because this is exactly how I was, whenever I was one of those forlorn Truth seekers. I had my hands strongly clamped around the steering wheel of life. I felt at that time, that if I let go of all the control I would wind up adrift in the world, lost like a piece of flotsam upon a bumpy wave. Yet the weird thing was, that as a result of this tiring control, I and my outer life always remained a mess and in a fragmented state. I felt separated from everyone, from the world at large and certainly from what I now call Reality.

It wasn't until I switched into Reality, and gave up all of the control over everything in my life, that life became progressively more enjoyable and peaceful. I then began to sense the Oneness of all life. Looking at life forms around me felt strangely like I was looking at myself. I could see the same life essence embedded within everything. Life literally came to life, whenever I let go and shifted my attention into the now. I realized that I shared this essence with everything. Indeed, in Reality I *actually* was this everything. It felt at times like I was dissolving into the air around me. I could see the sparkle of Spirit everywhere.

The clarity and crystal clear awareness, which arises whenever we allow the mental clutter to subside is truly wonderful. It is also a relief when we realize that the Spirit can turn our life into a more pleasing journey, whereas the controlling ego tends to suck all of the fun from life, and generally mucks it all up. It truly is a welcomed release to be able to give up the control, and then hand the reigns back over into the hands of Spirit, where they should have been all along.

Nonetheless, seekers seem to have an under riding belief that all is not well, and that they have innumerable inner demons to slay and problems to overcome, before they can let go and join in with the flow of life in this care free manner. However, is it any wonder this kind of belief is held, whenever we listen to some of the teachers out there, who seem hell bent on making us feel like we are not worthy of the Spirit. Even the new age crowd have the belief that we have dark corridors within ourselves, which we need to traverse before awakening can ever happen.

Even after many 'new agers' have turned their backs on organized religion, they might still feel it necessary to carry out some very religious practices, like renouncing the world to 'become' spiritually 'perfect'. Maybe we even feel that being 'perfect' is the only way to enlightenment or spiritual awakening. But let me ask you a simple question – do cats, dogs or birds worry about being perfect? Of course they don't; they are happy to be the carefree expression of life as it is, flowing with the moment, expressing themselves as nature and as the One intended.

You won't see your pet dog fasting or renouncing their bone. I don't think cats are into penance of any sort. I used to have a budgie, and I never once witnessed him begging any 'gods' to forgive him for being a miserable sinner. However, my budgie did occasionally bang his head on the bars of his cage, and more than once his head would bleed; maybe that was his attempt at flagellation, I can't be totally sure.

Let's take children now for an example. I'm pretty sure that you won't find many children beating themselves up for being 'imperfect'. Children are usually free of all that nonsense until the 'all-knowing' adults of the world inform them differently. Small children are already flowing in the moment with life's smooth current. That is of course, until the various education and belief systems of humanity 'educate' them to 'know' better.

Once we move into the egos world, out comes the list of do's and don'ts, out comes the rules and regulations of society and religion; the dictates, the demands and the suffocating pressure to 'become' what everyone else thinks we should become. We then begin to live the life of others, rather than to follow our own natural instincts and intuition, flowing with life in our own unique way. We enter the egos dreamland, and once

73

inside the egos prison house of thought we neglect the Spirit, as we try to 'become' something within the egos world.

We stop flowing with life and grip the steering wheel of life tightly, ever fearful that if we don't control everything, our world will crumble in around us. We forget that Spirit can render our experience in life to be perfect in all respects. But our trust in the Spirit usually gets smothered by the egos world of becoming, and it is that very _trust_ which has to be in place, before we can awaken to discover the flow of life and Oneness with the All.

All is well:

Awakening brings the realization that anything which we may deem to be 'bad' only emanates from being lost in the thought world. When we emerge from the thought world and come to life in the _Real_ world, our perception is that all is well. We then stop taking this temporary life so seriously.

Really, that's the main reason for many of the world's psychological and emotional problems – being lost in the thought world. Once lost inside the world of thought, we tend to take things far too seriously. We ignore the vibrancy of life which is within us and surrounding us. Whilst we are busy thinking and philosophizing about life, real life waits unbeknownst to us. It waits only for our invitation to allow life to be as it is. It dares us to peek out at the _Real_ world, to look out from under the heavy burden of the thought world, wherein is contained all of our fears, regrets, depressions, grudges, angers and all manner of neurosis. It asks us to choose simple Reality over dreamland and dare to consider that all can indeed be perceived to be well.

It is because we are taking a game far too seriously, that we don't see this. It is because of our seriousness, that we support the world's conflicts and find ourselves as slaves to the egos rat race. This game called 'life', which can become such a source of stress when directed by the ego, causes us this stress

74

and psychological pain, because we refuse to accept that this game meets with a _dead_ end, quite literally! At first glance it sounds like I am being downbeat in saying this, but I'm not really. This realization carries with it great liberation from all that is false, and from all that doesn't really matter at the end of the day. It means that we can play our game of life and enjoy it fully without attachment, demands or dependence upon a particular outcome, just the way we were meant to.

As we recognize that 'life' is only a game, the stress, effort, pain and seriousness goes out of it all. We no longer demand from life, and we no longer wait around refusing to be happy, until we 'become' what the ego has deemed to be a 'success'.

Maybe you disagree with me, maybe you think that the 'life on Earth' gig is a big serious thing, but you know, once awakened you probably won't see it that way because it's a bit hard to take the whole 'life on Earth' thing seriously, whenever you can see through it all as easily as you can see through a dirt-free windowpane. The ego tries to attract our attention with its little trinkets and trappings, and this is how it measures 'success' in life. Of course, the egos version of 'success' usually goes hand in hand with fear, anxiety, stress and feelings of worthlessness. At its worst, our life could become a living hell whenever we dance to the tune of the ego, and choose its world view over the Spirits. Really, at the end of the day, we shouldn't take life so seriously, because life doesn't take _us_ all that seriously!

After awakening, the whole 'life on Earth' thing is viewed as a passing show. You may be shocked as you will then see clearly how everyone is caught up in playing a game, which they don't recognize as being just a game. When you wake up from your trance of thought, you will still respond to the game, but then again you will still respond to losing money in a game of monopoly, but you aren't really fooled into thinking that the game is real, are you? Awakening out of dreamland leaves one viewing the so called problematic 'big serious life' in that manner. Problems then get a bit like losing money in a game of monopoly.

This is where going with the flow of life enters. When all of the struggle to become this or that ceases and we give up, surrendering to life's flow, releasing our hand from the control stick and then placing our trust in the Spirit to guide us, we usually find an ease and lightness in everything that we do. We also find that illusive better way of living, which the majority of humanity craves to find.

Making your life work:

Seekers are ceaselessly building up a 'process' - a process of endless spiritual 'becoming'. They are always trying to get to the now by avoiding the now - *"I will be in the now, sometime tomorrow"*. That is the underlying mantra of many spiritual aspirants. Some are really only interested in finding more and more methods of 'making their lives work'. Of course there is nothing wrong with that, but you have to realize that being awakened means that you tend to go with the flow of life.

Now, trying to 'make your life work' is not going with the flow. Trying to 'make your life work' involves exerting great effort and control over everything in life. But you cannot be in control of everything in life, and also leave it up to the flow- Spirit at the same time. Your hands are either on the steering wheel or off it. Awakening involves taking your hands off the steering wheel and joining your attention with life as it is. You mentally give up, surrender, throw in the towel and trust that your Spirit can guide you better than your heavy thought leaden mind could ever do.

This is when that trust is needed. It is also when the decision is finally made, between flowing with life and continuing to struggle within the egos suffocating world of 'becoming'. At first it seems as if you would be sacrificing your current lifestyle in order to choose awakening, but you wouldn't be. You would actually be enhancing your enjoyment of life. If what the ego offers leads to discontentment, stress and unhappiness then why would it be viewed as being a sacrifice to let it go? What good is it really, to gain the egos world but lose the peace within your own soul?

But it all depends upon what you want. Do you *really* want to enjoy every moment of simple life, or would you rather trade that enjoyment in for a life of pursuing what your ego thinks you need? Working simply because you feel a deep urge to do something for the sheer joy of doing it, is totally incomprehensible to the ego. The ego views this kind of natural activity as being wasted time. When you go with the flow of Spirit, then you will find that your natural interests and talents will begin coming to the surface of your awareness again. When this happens we don't feel the need to 'make our lives work', since when we follow our own passions and interests, our life is already 'working' the way it was meant to work, with fun and with ease.

I theorize that if we were all educated correctly to begin with, then these natural inclinations would be encouraged and watered so they could grow within us. If we were actually encouraged to pursue our own innate interests' then learning would be so much fun, and not only that, we would probably end up as being moderate Einstein's within the sphere of our fascination. We would then naturally go with the flow of life. But usually our natural talents and interests' are stamped out and put down by the world around us, as we play the egoic game of follow the leader.

I recall one such moment in my own life. I remember I was sitting in school one day during a class with a substitute teacher. I was thirteen years old, and I was flicking through a rather thick book I had borrowed from the library about the psychologist Sigmund Freud. I know it's a pretty strange thing to be reading at thirteen, but it interested me. Along came the teacher, and since the rest of the boys in the class were busy making noise and messing about, he stopped at my desk and asked what I was reading. So I told him, and his response was,

"You should put that psychology rubbish away, you won't get anywhere in this world with that, it's computers you want to be studying, that's where the real money is."

Then off he walked, and being young and easily influenced, I did as he said. I put the book away and wasted my time struggling with computers for a while (which I disliked). But hey, all of these years later the natural interest in psychology and many other natural interests are still there. Now, any decent teacher would've seen that I had a natural wiring for psychology and would've encouraged me to follow the path which I clearly loved. Years later, as I quit listening to know-it-all's and did follow my natural interests, I was able to start going with the flow of life. I was then able to finally let go of the struggle to 'become'. I gave up trying to 'make my life work' and I packed in the effort of trying to construct a better 'me'. Then I was able to live in Attentive Presence naturally and with ease, without effort or struggle, and life became a bit of an adventure as I flowed along doing the things I was naturally wired for. I done those things for the sheer fun they brought into my life, and for that reason only.

Only the thought leaden mind can interfere with our natural wiring. Only the thought leaden mind causes division, separateness, struggle, war and all of the darkness in our world. Our natural interests will never produce problems or stir up trouble, only the thought leaden mind will do that. Some of the greatest inventors of our time have had their inventions hijacked by the worlds' sleepwalkers, and only *then* were these inventions used for dire purposes, much to the dismay of the inventors themselves. The inventors were clearly going with the flow, but the sleepwalkers weren't. So now for example, we have nuclear or atomic energy being used inappropriately.

The Spirit appears willing to support our natural creature-hood, because then we are not going against the grain or introducing any effort; we are enjoying ourselves and what we are doing. We are then like creators, participating with life instead of fighting against it. That's what flowing with the Spirit

78

is all about; and that's when the effortlessness of awakening becomes very apparent.

Now, for awakening to have lasting effect you just have to go with the flow of life, and where the flow don't go you don't go, and it's as simple as that. You see, with awakening tomorrow does not often get a thought. Now don't get me wrong, you still keep a diary of appointments but the hectic mapping and controlling of life tends to fall away from you. Many people live their lives like this. They try to maintain a tight grip upon every aspect of their lives, and it's something which just *can't* be done without stress and anxiety being introduced. These people remind me of those showbiz guys who try to keep plates spinning on top of long poles. If there are too many plates spinning, it gets impossible to keep them all balanced, and then we find stress being introduced.

With awakening you stop controlling, you quit chasing, you cease wanting and you begin to recognize that all is well, because then all is indeed well within your being. That feeling realization is then extended out and into your world, making your outer world agreeable to you also. The old dissatisfied egoic mentality that once _refused_ to be happy until it had a fancy car or X amounts of money just doesn't have a voice that you would want to listen to anymore. You can still drive a fancy car and earn big money, don't get me wrong, I'm not suggesting that you should be driving an old rusty banger, or go around the place with holes in the backside of your trousers. However, once awake you won't be acquiring these things with an inferior need to make yourself feel good anymore. Your good feeling will be coming from within. It will be coming from the Spirit, and not from outside, and you will understand that nothing from the outside could ever make your life feel as sunny as the Spirit can.

There are many teachers out there, who will teach you how to take firm control of yourself and your life. They will teach you how to make a new ego for yourself. They have five year plans, lists of goals and targets to reach. They want you to delve into your unconscious to relive past hurts, to heal your inner child and to program your mind to 'become' a better 'you'. Yet all the while, the unconscious suggestion from this kind of activity is that you are currently not good enough. They don't seem to realize that past hurts, mistakes and bad experiences can bring a lot of wisdom in their wake. The effect of these past hurts can sometimes cause us to be willing to let go into the moment, and surrender to the flow of life. The influence of our 'past hurts' can be released in the present moment; however it requires for us to allow our awareness to clear.

A spiritual teacher I once visited made a very powerful statement, he said to me, *"living in the present puts an end to the past, and it dissolves all of your past hurts automatically"*. Now try telling some of the 'make your life work' teachers that. I call these teachers the 'make your life work' brigade. The 'make your life work' brigade are generally a very decent kind of breed. They are trying to help people improve their lot in life and that's good, but they have now infiltrated the spiritual seeking world. What they teach sometimes brings in an element of the universal source energy, and many Truth seekers are attracted to their discourses. So what happens when _sincere_ Truth seekers are attracted to the 'make your life work' brigade?

Once attracted, the seeker usually stops seeking within and they cast their eyes _out_. They focus upon the exterior life, and lose all focus of the interior life. They forget that when the interior is enlivened, then the exterior automatically follows and gets enlivened also. They lose sight of that pure realization, which they were really interested in from the outset. Yet apparently seekers are interested in the Spirit and knowing it intimately within their own experience. But if you get caught up with the 'make your life work' brigade, then you will most assuredly get distracted from awakening. You will also get distracted from going with the flow of life, which is so intrinsic to spiritual awakening.

I am often faced with the 'make your life work' brigade, and they are generally a nice bunch of people. However they don't appear to be at all interested, whenever I try to explain to them that I like to go with the flow of life. It's almost as if they misunderstand what I am saying; taking it to mean that I prefer to sit around all day sunbathing or strolling up and down the local seaside promenade like a beach bum. They don't want to listen when I tell them that I do indeed _act_ upon the guidance or intuition I receive, and I don't just wait around for some unseen hand to carry out the actions for me. So I find it easier to tell these guys, _"look mate, I go with the flow, and where the flow don't go, I don't go"_.

You see, I perceive that all is well within my world, and I have an innate knowing which allows me to know that all is going to remain well within my world. I realize that my exterior world is experienced according to the state of my inner nature. Now, my inner nature is in alignment with my true nature as Spirit. Therefore, I perceive the exterior world as being that which is the very same One thing as my inner essence. I am no longer bound by the hypnotic spell of thought, so therefore, I am no longer trying to run away from any inferior feelings, nor do I feel the need to 'become' something that I am not. I don't have the _want_ anymore, to 'become' something which has been formed by societies clone like thinking. I can't see the point in maintaining an illusory ego or an outward face which is sterile and practiced, just so the world will maybe think some good thoughts about me. I no longer care what the world thinks about me, because it only matters what I think, since what I think is the only thing which has any power to alter my perception of the world I know.

The realization of the One is that _all is well_, and we then see the world according to that perception. Yes even when problems arise, all is still well. Problems are taken care of to the best of our ability, but they no longer cause us mental turmoil. So when we see and feel that all is well, then we don't feel the need any longer to fix what we once thought of as being un-well. In short, we no longer perceive anything as being broken, so we don't feel the need to fix what we cannot see as being broken.

So therefore, we don't see that we need to 'make our lives work', because we know first-hand that the only reason we ever felt the need to 'make our lives work', was because we were saturating our awareness with thoughts of an inferior and lacking quality. When those thoughts are ignored and we allow instead the emergence of the Spirit; then that perception of inferiority and lack is gone. The abundant perception of the One gets projected into our world, and it is then that we will feel that all is well.

When some people hear this they usually say, *"what about war, poverty and famine; that's not okay."* They are right of course. There are still problems in the world to be solved, but the perception that 'all is well' approaches these 'problems' and doesn't get emotional or stressed about them. A clear perception sees how to solve problems without using those problems as an excuse for worry, stress or insanity. The mind-set which has created many of the world's problems is not the same mind-set that will solve them. With awakening, we look not only for the solution to problems, but we look at the cause also, so the problem can then be eradicated for all time. This includes problems on a personal level.

Now, someone once said to me, whenever they realized that my priority interest was in awakening to Reality; *"Ach, all of these spiritual guys, chasing after spirits whilst letting their lives go to waste"*. Now, it seems to be the case that those who have released their grip from the steering wheel of life and have allowed themselves to awaken to Reality, all find that going with the flow of life works much better than trying with effort to 'make your life work'. By going with the flow you enjoy all aspects of life, and no longer demand anything from life. You no longer have that clingy, needy and impoverished state of mind which once made you feel so small. So I don't know about you, but I *can't* call that letting your life go to waste. However, I would call living your life in total dissatisfaction and stress - letting your life go to waste!

Now, your life will never 'work' whilst you remain in stress, and it doesn't matter how much money you make throughout your life because with that stressful, demanding and dissatisfied attitude of mind, you will never be able to enjoy life anyway. You'll be too busy coping with your stress. Now, that is _not_ making your life work - that is ruining your life. All the same, whilst going with the flow we have to be alert to the inspiration and urges we may receive. And when we do receive it, we have to _act_ upon it. Nonetheless, if you know that you are not _truly_ going to surrender and flow with Reality and the Spirit, then stick to the 'make your life work' brigade because who knows, what they teach may eventually work for you. The guys who teach the hundred ways to a better 'you' stuff will certainly think so anyway!

7

Dialogues 1

Q: *What is the point in us having a body, work, children or relationships if it is only our spiritual nature that matters?*

A: The reason why the spiritual nature matters the most, is because what we have going on within us, is what we experience as our world or 'my life'. We will always experience life in accordance with what is going on within our awareness. Therefore, it is imperative that we keep our inner mental space healthy, clean and clear. We are either projecting thought or seeing what's real. Therefore if we keep our awareness clear of unreal thought scenarios, we get to see what's real and are no longer experiencing a world of make believe, or a world of fear, malice and hatred etc. We experience the world as it is, because we are operating from Truth and no longer from thoughts dreamed up in our mind.

As for the point in work, children or relationships; well these things will still go on, and as a result of approaching these things with awareness of what's real, we will enjoy them more fully. We then approach everything (work included) with an unattached frame of mind. Awakening releases us to experience life in a care free manner.

Don't forget that the One is not only within us; it is also within the apparent 'others' we see. When we are in touch with Truth, we perceive the Truth of others also. We will no longer react so much to what we think of others, since we will know the

Truth instead. But don't me wrong, this also doesn't mean that we are going to like the mind-set of everyone we meet. Once awake, we may find that we no longer have any desire to share company with certain people, simply because we will no longer be on the same wave length as them. We may know the Truth, but we are also going to be faced with the conditioned mind-set of others also. If someone is heavily steeped in egoic consciousness, then we won't have much in common with them, even though we will still recognize that we are all made of the same 'stuff'.

Q: Sometimes I feel that if I could only get away from the busy world, then awakening would be easier.

A: I understand what you mean. Sometimes it can feel like that, but try to realize that we don't need to give up everyday life for awakening to occur; this has been a misunderstanding within the world for millennia. That's why many people went to live like hermits. They felt that they needed to give up worldly life to awaken to Truth. They also felt that they had to deny the body any sort of physical comfort. The body is part of our experience in this world; if the Spirit didn't want this experience then it wouldn't happen. So the Spirit clearly wants to engage in, and fully enjoy the whole 'life on planet Earth' scenario.

Once awake, I found that I didn't need to give up this, or deny that. I only had to stay clear enough for the Truth to dawn upon my awareness. When that awakening happened, I found that I actually embraced life more fully, since I made no more demands upon it. I could let life be as it is, leaving me to accept each and every moment just as it is, without prejudice, stress, hatred, fear, greed or any of the many mental afflictions associated with the egoic 'me' and its thought spell.

Q: How do we know that the only thing which is real is Spirit?

A: The Real pervades everything; the world and the universe. We are the same source manifesting as that everything. Awakening involves the realization that I am the all; I am the One. Reality at its most subtle is a unified field of energy from which we derive our being. The scientists who study quantum physics know this now as a fact. Some scientists call this field the Zero Point field. They know it holds a source of immense power. It has been called by many names. It has been called the Tao, Nirvana, the Kingdom of Heaven or simply God. We could go on with the names and labels ascribed to it, but the realization in awareness is the important thing.

When that realization hits the awareness, then we understand that we *are* that unified field of energy, *we are that*, we are not apart or separate from it. Only experiential realization of this is what is required. Once we have this realization, we will no longer be totally fooled by appearances, nor will our thoughts seem as serious and substantial as they once appeared to be. You see, we usually accept every thought we have as being a correct interpretation of reality, but thought contaminates reality. Pure awareness is devoid of all interpretations (positive or negative) and demands or alterations made upon the moment of Reality's now. Therefore the *Real* can only be experienced in awareness when we let go of the un-real from our awareness. Now, thought is the un-real.

Q: My thoughts torment me sometimes, usually at night when I'm lying in bed.

A: That's only because you believe your thoughts to be true and real. You take them seriously because you don't realize that you can shake off the hypnotic effect of those thoughts, just by seeing them for the mirage which they are. When you see through them for the illusion which they really are, you might actually find yourself laughing that you once took them so seriously. It's at that point when they more or less dissolve from the awareness and cease to arise as much as they used to.

Q: *How do I see through them?*

A: Take your attention beyond them. Or, if you are lying in bed, then just observe the thoughts as they come and go. Be the unattached witness. Don't judge them or beat yourself up for having them; just watch, witness, observe and after a short while you'll notice that _you_ are not those thoughts, but rather, you are the observer, the witnessing consciousness or the unattached awareness.

When awareness is saturated in thought, it seems like those thoughts are very serious and real. Like when we are sleeping at night and we are having a nightmare, the nightmare seems very real and the body will even react to that dream as if it were a real experience. The heart beats faster, the blood pressure goes up, we start to sweat and stress hormones will even shoot through the bloodstream. Yet this very physical effect is taking place because of our reaction to an un-real dream. Only when we wake up, do we realize that it wasn't real and we say to ourselves, *"phew, thank God that was only a dream"*.

But, there is another state called lucid dreaming. In lucid dreaming we realize that we are dreaming whilst we are still asleep. We look around in the dream and we know that it is not real, even though it is still a normal type of dream, with people, props and settings. We might even say to ourselves within the dream, *"Oh, this is just a dream I'm having"*. Now, when we are dreaming lucidly we won't react to any scary stuff that might occur within the dream, simply because we know it is a dream and is therefore not real. This is a good way to describe what awakening is like. We no longer react to thoughts, because we see them in the same way as a lucid dreamer sees his dream as not real. We are therefore no longer affected by the dream or by thoughts.

Q: Yes, and in those lucid dreams I've noticed that I wake up very quickly after realizing I'm asleep and dreaming.

A: It's the same with spiritual awakening. How can thought continue to saturate your awareness, whenever you have seen through it all and have found it to be an un-real dream? When you take your attention out of the dream, awareness is able to see through the dream, or shake the dream off. Awareness or the witnessing observer then sees the dream for what it really is, which is nothing but a mere dream, a trick created by thought. The awakened see thoughts in the same manner and therefore no longer take them seriously. Therefore, we are no longer a victim of thought, and so we can finally let thought go, including the thoughts which create that separate sense of 'me' in the awareness.

Q: But surely we need thought?

A: We don't need it as much as you would suppose. Have you noticed that most of our good ideas just seem to come from nowhere, usually at a time when our mind is quiet? We certainly don't need dopey daydreams running in our mind all day either. Now, our current problem is that we have become so identified with our thoughts, that we can no longer tell the difference between thought and Reality. We also mistake this tool of thought to be what we are. We create an identity made from thought, then we unknowingly hypnotize our awareness with that thought created identity and we tell the world, *"I am what I think I am"*. But here's the thing; we are most definitely not and never will be what we think we are!

Q: How can we attend to Reality whenever we are leading a busy life? I can't find enough quiet time to become present.

A: Look, it does not matter whether you are a busy person, or whether you are a total slacker. The One is in all situations and in all places. It all depends upon where your attention is at. Is your attention locked up in dreamland or is it placed firmly in the here and now? The One is always here and now, it is nowhere else. It is certainly not tomorrow or next week, and it does not rely upon you sitting in some quiet desolate place in order to realize it. The One is there within your busy work place, and also within your quiet church; it is there when your two year old child is kicking and screaming, and it is there when you are wrapped in deep meditation. The One is everywhere and is prevalent throughout the world and the universe at all times.

It really is only a matter of where your attention is focused. Is your attention split between the here and now, and what you _think_ of the here and now? Your thoughts and beliefs will always contaminate the here and now, thereby contaminating your true Reality.

Q: But if you live a quiet life, then you haven't got as much going on. So that should make it easier to be present, shouldn't it?

A: No, not necessarily so. Living an idle life could lead you to spin thought dra..as more so, than if you were a busy person. Busy people usually don't have enough time to be spinning lots of silly little dramas in their mind. Someone who lives an idle life will seek for entertainment to relieve their boredom. Now what better way to relieve boredom, than to start dreaming up all manner of weird thought dramas inside your mind?

What makes awakening easier, is to merely have the desire for it. You have to be 100% willing to let go of your thought dramas, that's all. Once that willingness is in place, then living with Attentive Presence becomes simple. I used to think that I had to live a very quiet and boring life in order to awaken, so for a long time I lived a very sheltered kind of lay monks existence. Of course, this was when I was hypnotized by false assumptions which I received at the hands of some of those well-meaning 'spiritual' teachers we have out there.

We are conditioned to believe that when the realization of Truth dawns upon us, we will then live sedentary lives with no action anymore. We also believe that we will hear trumpets sounding and see fireworks blazing. This of course is unbridled nonsense. It leads us to believe that awakening is a super 'achievement' and requires for us to live a boring life to 'attain' it.

I found that all I had to 'do' was simply to listen to life as it was happening all around me. I listened with _attention_ to all of the sounds I was making as I worked, or to the sound of traffic as I walked along a busy street. If I was reading, I would pay full attention to the words, being careful not to let my mind drift off into dreamland. If I was talking to someone, I listened to them fully and also to the sound of my own voice as I spoke. I would mainly listen to life, but I would also deliberately feel, see, smell and taste life too. If I was eating, I would deliberately focus on the taste of the food. If I was walking through a forest park, I would take in the smell of the pine trees, or maybe the smell of a barbecue in the distance or whatever else arose. I would feel the wind as it brushed past my face, or notice the warmth of the sun beating down on me.

This diverted my attention away from thought, and took me deeply into the now. So, this is what it really means to live in the now, or to live with Attentive Presence. Then I noticed that thought gradually loosened its grip, and a great sparkle and crystal clear unifying clarity began to emerge in my awareness. As a result, I now see what is, rather than what I think is.

Q: So do you not take any quiet time to meditate or practice relaxation?

_A:_ When people ask me if I meditate I tell them, _"Yes, 24 hours a day, 7 days a week"_. Since meditation is really all about taking your attention beyond thought and uncovering Reality, then strictly speaking you *could* call Attentive Presence a form of meditation. But as for making time for *formal* meditation in the hope of achieving a 'spiritual' goal in the future, well, I would have to say that I don't formally meditate anymore. Though I do have a short power nap most afternoons which I find to be deeply relaxing, but I don't see any need to get into any funny sitting positions or to formalize it in any way, since I'm just having a bit of a rest really.

There are a few cats which have made my back garden their home, and every time I look out, they are also having a nap. It's funny though; when I watch them having their afternoon nap, I don't get the impression that they are being very formal about it. Cats like to relax in the afternoon and so do I, mainly because it gives an energy boost, that's all there really is to it.

Q: But do you not use any mental techniques when you are relaxing like this?

A: I try to live in Attentive Presence at all times, even when I'm having a nap. Now that's the best way to stay relaxed. But when I'm napping, instead of paying attention through the senses, I close my eyes and pay attention within my mind. I simply observe or watch any lingering thoughts which might be floating about; observing them as they come and go. I'm just watching that voice in the head in an unattached manner. These days it doesn't say very much however. That voice doesn't seem to like being observed, it tends to quieten down all on its own as I bring attention to it. So, then the mind naturally clears, and I find that a great depth of relaxation envelopes the body, which is rather nice, since I like the energy boost I gain from this short power nap.

Now, if you *do* use meditation or a form of relaxation, then by all means continue to use it if you are gaining some benefit from that. We all know that formal meditation has a lot of benefits just as physical exercise has, but awakening is a different kettle of fish altogether. For example; what happens to your awareness throughout the day?

Attentive internal observation is helpful though, since it gives great insight into how thought can hypnotize the awareness, since whilst you are observing thought you see clearly the dreamlike effect it has upon your awareness. You then notice how when you are not paying attention, your mind can get saturated in these dreamlike thought scenarios. You will then understand exactly how the mind really works, and how madness can hypnotize the mind quite easily if you are not paying careful attention to Reality. You'll begin to notice first-hand the difference between thought and Reality. Like I said, it gives great insight into how thought operates. Now, if you want to call that a technique, then so be it. I don't call it a technique. I call it having a nap with Attentive Presence.

Q: What does it really mean to be spiritually awake?

A: It means that your life experience gets spiritualized. You see what is Real. It means that you regain your natural state of sanity, since being lost in thought is the cause of the entire world's insanity. It means that you are awakened to the true nature of your Spirit, and also the outer Reality of everything which is the same Spirit. You realize that all is One. You are the all; you are the One. Sometimes it can take your breath away, but it's mostly about keeping your inner space clean of unwanted thoughts and aligning your attention with the Real instead.

The awakened recognize the un-reality of thought, and as a result of that recognition they don't take it all so seriously anymore. Therefore it's rather difficult to take what people perceive as being an 'ordinary life' seriously anymore. You'll be 'in the world but not of the world'. Have you heard that old statement before – *In the world but not of the world?* It means that you can enjoy the ride, but don't really give a damn about the outcome. To most folks, you'll be seen as being somewhat strange for not giving a hoot about all of the strife everyone else gets so enmeshed in, but what they think won't matter to you any longer.

It's like when you read a novel; you can get deeply engrossed in the book as you are reading it. You feel the characters emotions and you enjoy the story, but all along you know it is only a story and has absolutely no reality at all. You are un-attached, free and at ease. Awakening is a bit like that. Life gets a bit like watching a movie or reading a novel. You will still take pleasure in it, but you find it very hard to take any aspect of it seriously anymore. It is the ultimate freedom; all of the stress and emotional problems you once had which came from being so spellbound in your thought story, go straight out the window. Once the un-reality of the thought story is recognized, the burden from that thought story simply drops away from you. It's just like dropping a heavy weight you didn't even know you were carrying.

People everywhere are trying to relax nowadays, but if they dropped their thought story and lived life with Attentive Presence, then that relaxation would be automatic. However, that doesn't mean that you will end up being distant from life, or immune to the flow of life's changing current. It just means that things won't get you down, or stress you out too much either. Nonetheless, when you see others taking their thought story seriously, it will make you shake your head in disbelief. You may reach a point when you will want to vigorously shake those people, and tell them that the story they saturate their mind with is not real at all.

Q: How did awakening change you, or make you different?

A: Awakening is only about waking up and seeing the Truth; it's not about changing yourself or trying to become different. I am one who simply prefers to align my attention with life as it is presented to me, moment by moment. I no longer want to be trapped in thought dramas, since I found all of that to be very tiring, upsetting and quite a bore. I can't be bothered with spinning lots of little thought stories inside my head anymore. Once upon a time that kind of thing entertained me, but then it all got out of hand and I *finally* decided to let it go.

So, the weight I had sitting upon my shoulders fell away as I began to live in Attentive Presence. I then began to feel real light, weightless, almost bouncy, and my world brightened up. A very sharp clarity arose in my perception and I then began to feel the Oneness of life. When I look at the world around me, it feels like everything is alive and has its own character, even trees, grass and water. I sense that I am looking at myself as I look around me; there's a dissolving into everything a lot of the time, it fluctuates though. Thoughts still come and go, just not as much as they used to, and anyway I now let them go, whereas beforehand I would've clung to them. I now prefer Reality over thought, ease over strife and going with the flow of life over constant effort. It doesn't mean that the awakened are special, like many believe. In fact, you could awaken right now if you honestly desired it as much as I did.

Q: What about wisdom - did awakening make you wiser?

A: Anyone who has the ability to learn from their life experience, their mistakes and the mistakes of others is one who holds the keys to wisdom. The wisdom gained through awakening is the ability to see through the thought show. Then you will know the difference between Truth and illusion. You see, wisdom comes from experience unlike knowledge which mainly comes from books and teachers. We have been conditioned to believe that the awakened are all knowing and all wise; that's a lot of rubbish though. The awakened still make mistakes; however, they are able to learn lessons from making those mistakes.

I don't see myself as being a 'wise' guy. Some so called 'un-awakened' people are far better at playing the whole 'life on earth' gig better than I am, so that makes them wiser in my eyes.

94

I can't do anything apart from go with the flow of life, and run with whatever life presents to me moment to moment, but when I need advice in a particular field I ask for it from those who can give it, even if they are sound asleep in their dreams. So, nobody is all 'knowing' and all 'wise', and guess what, neither is your favourite guru.

Q: So, even after awakening, we still need advice?

A: Yes we do. Once awakened from the thought spell, you will know that we are all dream characters playing a little game here, but you won't know everything there is to know about that game. I'm sure you'll still want to play a good game, so you'll need to take good advice from those who are well versed in what you require. To me these people are like the One showing me what's next. I just follow the clues and the answers which the One gives me. However, those clues and answers do come in very mysterious ways sometimes.

The answers I need usually come through a deep hunch I feel arising within me, but sometimes my directions can come through a book, the television, another person or even sometimes a child has given me the next clue I need. I listen, I pay attention to life and I follow the clues, then I take *action*. The action part is always natural and effortless though, even if it requires that I work at something for weeks, months or years. I always have fun operating this way. That's basically how you live your life in the flow. You stay alert, so you will recognize any guidance as it comes (by whatever means) and then you move into effortless action.

Q: Do you still live a normal life?

A: Of course I do, I'm not weird you know. I still do all of those things which you and others like to do. I work, I go for walks, I exercise, I play golf, I watch movies and I read novels too. Also, if a hammer hits my finger - *guess what* - I might let out a hollering yelp, mixed with an obscenity or two. Nobody would know that I was even interested in awakening until I started talking about it. By the way, I don't usually talk much about it at all, unless I'm asked about it, mainly because people get all kinds of funny ideas into their heads about how you should be acting after awakening. Many hold childish pictures in their minds of stereotype saints, and then think that's what awakening looks like. I couldn't be bothered explaining my position to people anymore, that's why I wrote it all down in a book. Life goes on and I choose to live it in freedom, so I don't bow to the funny ideas others have concerning how the awakened should act.

Q: What's it like to be awake?

A: Awakening liberates you from much fear and anxiety, simply because fear and anxiety is nothing but thought, and you will then have moved beyond thought. Seeing your essence in everything frees you in a way that you can't understand, until you surrender to the flow of life yourself. The word 'awakened' is only a useful word to distinguish between the two different states of consciousness; awake and asleep.

Do you want to know what awakening is really like? Well it's like being *free*, that's really the best word I have to describe it. Now, can your mind imagine that; complete and utter freedom? It's freedom from all of the boring, joyless and stuffy spiritual-religious rules. It's freedom from stress, depression, anxiety and the effort of unending becoming. It is freedom to embrace your natural character and play the game of life like it should be played, with passionate fun. But it's also most importantly about coming to know your true nature as that One indivisible unity. Words however will *never* touch this. You have to allow the great clarity of awakening to emerge within yourself to understand it properly.

Q: What do you mean when you talk about the natural genetic character?

A: Being part of a large family, I have always noticed many similarities in character, tastes and interests running through my family and that of other families. Not everyone is exactly the same, that's not what I'm saying. It's just that there appears to be similarities which pop up a lot from one generation to the next. Now, some scientists theorize and have more or less proven that through our genetics we inherit a base personality, or a particular flavour of character. Well, according to scientific findings, the natural genetic character is derived from genetic wiring which you inherited through birth. All of those *natural* tendencies, interests, attractions and passions; they appear to be built upon genetic inheritance and influence, which we then build upon. Of course some will disagree with this, but there is a growing body of scientific evidence to back it up.

I've noticed that Spirit appears to use this genetic wiring to play the game of life, whenever we accept fully our natural genetic character and go with the flow of the moment. It appears that we only ever feel like we are going against the grain or embarking upon an uphill struggle, whenever we are pursuing something which is not in line with our inbuilt genetic character.

But the genetic character is still only a role we are playing. It's natural because it's what our body is wired with, so to speak. It's the experience we as Spirit are seeking to have. But this genetic character isn't totally *real*. What we truly are is something else entirely. Our true inner self is not wholly subject to this genetic wiring, but neither does it oppose it. Instead Spirit will embrace wholesome attributes of the genetic character. Now, the wholesome attributes of the genetic character, are those traits which bring true creative delight into our lives. People like Ford, Einstein, Tesla or Freud were very much flowing in line with their true character; that's why they were geniuses.

Q: *So what's the difference between ego and the genetic character then?*

A: When I use the word ego then I am referring to a thought based sense of 'me' which is not the natural character. The ego is something which we are trying to 'become' because we cannot accept our natural character just as we are. The ego to my mind is hypnosis of sorts. It's what we believe that we are, based upon the worlds influence and conditioning. When we awaken, we see through all phenomena, not only the ego but the genetic character as well. We then know that we are pure life. But we need something to play the game of life on planet Earth, don't we?

You see the natural character will always be in line with what brings happiness and passion; whereas the ego will find itself doing things mainly for prestige, to outdo others or to be seen as being the kingpin. The ego goes against the grain and causes life to be stressful. It has you doing things in life which you hate, like working in a job which you dread. It opposes the flowing river of life. The ego is what I *think* I am, and what I *think* I should be, so the world will accept me as one of its own. It subjugates itself to conformity. So ego is thought based, and it is always trying to alter the natural character, so it can fit in with societies clone like conditioning.

Now, one in touch with the natural character will only dance to their own tune. However, that doesn't mean they will be a rebel, but only that they will be free. With the natural character, you will feel a strong urge to do certain things in life. These things may make you a lot of money or they may not, but you won't be doing them with money on your mind, you'll be doing them for the sole reason of enjoying yourself. You could work at those natural urges all day and all night and never get tired. You'll find yourself with many varied interests which you'll find to be naturally fascinating. The natural character might follow a life as an artist, a teacher or a musician, but it could also follow a life as a stock trader, a business man or a world leader.

Q: After awakening, could the natural character still do bad?

A: The natural character could follow a life of anything at all, but generally, once awakened, you won't find yourself doing things that are detrimental to the world, simply because you'll be beyond thought dramas, which are the only thing which can ever cause detriment to the world. That's the beauty of awakening. You don't have to try to be good, you will end up naturally aligned with what we call good, though it won't be the stereotypical 'good' which the religions try to imitate. You'll play your natural role, and then you are no longer a hindrance to others or the world anymore.

At first, you may find that societies clone like mind-set might oppose you going your own way and being natural. Some may even hate you for no longer toeing the line of religion or of society's brain washing. Many famous scientists and philosophers were fiercely attacked and slandered, simply because they stepped away from the egos world and found their own truth naturally within.

But even when flowing with your natural role; all the while you are totally aware that a role is all it is. Once awakened you won't become lost in it, or identify with the role you are playing in any way. You then look upon the other actors on the stage, and to your awakened mind they look like they are totally hypnotized with the role they are playing. They identify with the character and get lost in the characters story, believing that the play they are involved in is real, and so they cannot distinguish between what is real and what is un-real. On the other hand, one who is awakened can easily distinguish between what is real and what is un-real.

Q: There seems to be a big difference between the awakened natural self, and the un-awakened ego.

A: Yes, there is. An un-awakened person is one who mechanically reacts to every thought which passes through their mind. They are puppets being manipulated at all times by the strings of thought. They are unable to tell the difference between thought and Reality. To the un-awakened, thought is their reality and they usually never question this so called 'reality' at all. To the un-awakened mind, those who do question the un-reality of the world's thought story are seen as being somewhat mad or weird. Now what a strange situation we are in, whenever insanity views sanity as being madness, yet this is what we are faced with; the insane view the sane as being mad. Now who could possibly find agreement in such a world?

Going with the flow of whatever appeals to you *naturally*, is seen as being a haphazard way of living life to one who is stuck in their ego. It is seen as being madness, because to the ego you have to plan every little thing in life. The ego wants a five year plan and all of that. The ego doesn't do things because they feel good; it usually has fear of the future, feelings of lack or outdoing others on its mind. Yet going with the flow of your natural character will always feel right, good and easy. You'll also enjoy what you are doing, unlike when you do egoic things, which usually winds up making you feel stressed and despondent; like life is a big uphill struggle.

Q: So, we should just accept our natural self, whatever way we find it to be?

A: Yes, but be sure to keep your mind devoid of thought dramas, and be attentive to the moment or you will drift into the un-natural state of being spellbound by your thought story. The thought story is not natural, only pure awareness is natural, and then from that pure awareness your natural character is free to come alive. Then you will be free from stress, anxiety and the many mental afflictions associated with being stuck in dreamland.

100

The way I see it is quite simple really. If we keep our own mind clear of upsetting thought dramas, then we would no longer be harming anyone else, because we would no longer be mentally harming ourselves. We would naturally be at peace within ourselves. That peace would then be extended out and into the world. This is the only way that the world will truly be at peace. The inner peace has to be allowed firstly, otherwise whatever so called 'peace' the world experiences will end up being very short lived. Now, this peace does not require a religious or 'spiritual' list of do's and don'ts. It only requires that we allow our awareness to remain clear and free in the ever present now. But, I guess it all matters what you yourself feel about this. Do you *really* want to be free, or do you want to be a slave to someone else's opinion of how you should be?

Q: Well, I suppose we would all like to be free.

A: Well that's great; then accept yourself as you are, without all of that head stuff which turns your life into a stressful episode of becoming. Only the head stuff like the spiritual rules and the interfering thought dramas need to be let go of. But it's all just thought at the end of the day, trying to keep your mind spinning out of control. These thought dramas try to lock you into a prison, where the prison bars are made of beliefs, philosophies, religious rules and the effort of unending becoming.

You only have to stop letting that voice in your head ruin your life. Don't listen to it when it says that you are not good enough, or that you have to become this or that. Give that voice the boot. Accept yourself fully, and to hell with what the world and others think of you. Live your life the way you want to. Do the unique things that you want to do, pursue your own interests and passions and play your game of life just the way that you were uniquely wired to play it. Accept yourself as you are, and live each day with Attentive Presence. Now that's the real key to your spiritual and mental freedom.

8

The Spiritual Search

The end of the search:

These days there are a growing number of people who have spent many years *honestly* searching for spiritual realization, and they have found their search amounting to nothing but a dead end. They are confused, and they are also frustrated with the many different philosophies and contradictory enlightenment prescriptions available in the world today. I've come across many who say that they are sick of the continuous search, and claim that they want to mark an end to it all; and this is without even finding that realization which they were initially seeking for. This seems like a pity to me.

Many have allowed their minds to become so overstuffed with various concepts, philosophies and beliefs that they cannot even see it is this very accumulation of concept, philosophy and belief which makes awakening appear forever distant. Philosophy was only meant to point towards Reality, it was not meant to act like a prison of thought where we end up like a dog chasing its own tail. In the beginning of the spiritual search we do indeed need a little philosophy to point the way, but why is it more often than not, that we get caught up in chasing down more and more philosophies, rather than getting on with the business of awakening?

Indeed, many seekers appear to indulge so much in conceptual thinking and philosophy, they find it quite easy to talk the awakened talk, but when it comes to walking the walk (or actual awakening), well, they appear to have overlooked that. Now, I understand that a lot of seekers are not necessarily seeking Reality or awakening at all, but many instead prefer to take comfort in their beliefs and concepts. However, these are not the kind of seekers I speak of, when I say there are many who want to call an end to the search. These types will merrily search forever, but the other kind of seeker (the sincere seeker) will not be satisfied with a nicely packaged philosophy or a collection of 'wise' sounding concepts. The sincere seeker desires _realization_, and that alone. These are the ones who have most likely put their entire lives on hold in search of awakening.

There is no doubt that if we are true to our desire for awakening, then our search will definitely come to an end someday. But that will be the day, on which we will know for certain that we have found what it is we have been seeking for. On that day, we may feel like giving ourselves a good slap in the face for being so asleep, that we missed the sheer simplicity of awakening for all of these years. We will then realize that we have spent all of our time and effort seeking Reality like a bird in search of the sky. Now this can be a very weird moment of realization.

I recall the moment when this simplicity struck me. I found myself sitting down and shaking my head, almost in disbelief that I had spent so much time, money and effort only to discover that what I was seeking for was here and now, already present, within me and all around me and I just wasn't paying any attention to it. Of course, I had heard the philosophy of it lots of times before that moment, but it never sunk in until I was _finally_ ready to let go and embrace the eternal now. In my mind, it all became so simple at that moment. In all situations I then began to choose Reality over the daydream.

I let go of the mental clutter with _each moment_. Funny enough, most of this clutter was many of the spiritual philosophies I had satiated my mind with over the years. Now

103

with a new clear seeing, I recognized that much of the philosophy I had once used as a spiritual crutch was a lot of old rubbish – and that is putting it very mildly indeed. To live fully in the moment, I no longer needed philosophy, and I understood that it only ever got in the way anyhow. You see, no philosophy can contain the Truth, not even nondual philosophy, because philosophy is derived from thought and belief, and the Truth is arrived at by moving beyond thought and belief.

Now, because I was interested in what it truly meant to get *real*, I found myself beginning to let go of a lot of the beliefs I had once cherished, since when we discover the Truth, then we also uncover the lies as well. Since my beliefs were constructed from mere thought, I could then see through the spellbinding influence which belief held upon my awareness. Now, this can be a pretty shaky time, if one is not sincere about their intention to be 100% free in absolute Reality.

I found that my spiritual dreamland gave way to Attentive Presence through the weight of my desire and readiness to allow the moment to be what it is, without thought contamination. Awakening cannot last any longer than a mere momentary experience, without that *readiness* to allow the outer world to remain what it is. We need to surrender our tendency to fall into mental turmoil over everything 'bad' that apparently happens. When that readiness to surrender is in place, we will find our search naturally ending, and then the awakening should follow soon.

Frustration with the search is usually a sign that awakening is around the corner. However, the search will not end in frustration and then remain at frustration indefinitely. The search ends when we find, and if we are indeed sincere about it, the Spirit will compel us until we *do* find. We simply cannot say, *"I'm quitting the search"*, because it will not happen that way, no matter how much we like to think we are in charge of this. We will just have no choice in the matter, since it is not the ego which seeks awakening. Awareness or Spirit seeks to break free from the prison of thought, to know and recognize itself once again. And when the Spirit has a willing receptacle with which it can bring forth awakening, then the Spirit will eventually have what the Spirit wants.

Spiritual teachers & philosophy:

Disillusionment with various teachers will be the first sign of the search coming to its eventual climax. We will begin to see through the 'mystical' charade which some 'teachers' exhibit. Other spiritual seekers might then call us 'negative' as we call into question the integrity of certain teachers. We may find ourselves cast out into the cold as a result of our questioning. This disillusionment phase is not a nice thing to go through, however, it is indeed a *necessary* thing to go through if we are to ever fully wise up. This phase shouldn't last very long though; it all depends upon how daring we are to trust in our own inner guidance. Some might say that it all depends upon how *arrogant* we are, since paddling your own canoe to awakening can be viewed as being a rather arrogant thing to be doing.

But we should still remain open for any assistance or guidance we may receive from any _authentic_ teachers we encounter. So, how do we recognize an authentic teacher? Well, for a start, what they say will make absolute sense. There will be no hidden motive to keep you in the darkness of confusion either. There will be no air of holier-than-thou or specialness emanating from them. They will appear quite normal and will not at all be putting on the performance of being a mystically powered Superman/woman. An authentic teacher will know the terrain (so to speak). They tend to know all of the pitfalls and all of the snares one might encounter upon a spiritual search, and they are most likely not afraid to challenge any erroneous beliefs and philosophies we may be carrying. So an authentic teacher can therefore be of great assistance; if we are willing to listen to them that is.

Although, through the phase of disillusionment we could become so cynical about misleading teachers, that we may end up rejecting the authentic teachers as well. This is called *'throwing the baby out with the bath water'*. Simple and genuine teachers can help to make the transition from dreamland to Reality a much smoother ride. So you should accept sensible advice, warnings or good guidance when it comes, and try to keep an open mind - though not *so* open that your brains fall out!

I have been accused at times of being very cynical about some spiritual teachers and their teachings. Well, I have to admit that I am a little cynical about those who would lead _true_ innocent seekers upon a merry dance (which usually isn't so merry at the end of the day). Because the merry dance usually takes honest seekers away off on a tangent, into new age or seeming 'nondual' philosophies (which has become like religion in disguise). We can remain forever stuck in those philosophies if we are not careful. Some teachers would prefer that to happen though, as they would then get to play the role of the 'guru' indefinitely. If we aren't careful, we could wind up forgetting that our pure intention whenever we had originally set out upon the spiritual search was for absolute mental freedom and _direct realization_ of our true nature as Spirit or the One.

Now, saturating your mind with new age, nondual or religious philosophies and beliefs has nothing at all to do with Reality and uncovering your true nature. Reality has absolutely nothing whatsoever to do with what you think and believe. Dogs, cats and birds don't carry around beliefs, philosophies or worry about whether they are treading the right spiritual 'path'. Dogs, cats and birds live totally in the present without rules, regulations, beliefs, philosophies, mantras or spiritual taboos. They allow the flow of life or Spirit to move within them freely, activating their natural creature-hood. They are unencumbered by the religiosity we human beings get so entangled by.

We tend to think that our ability to conceptualize about the nature of our reality helps in spiritual awakening, but it actually interferes with it. Words are only useful to point towards Reality, however, if we get entangled in the words to the exclusion of an authentic awakening, then these words and philosophies become a trap. Furthermore, if it were not for our beliefs, conceptualization and our repetitive thinking, then we wouldn't have lost awareness of the Truth in the first place.

Our beliefs, concepts and philosophies are nothing more than thoughts putting on a show in our mind, playing tricks to give us the illusion of security or certainty. Thought has a tendency to hypnotize ones awareness with its content, and if you find yourself gaining comfort from your thought content, then it usually ends up as a set of beliefs.

Now, beliefs may be beneficial when they cause certain effects in your life, like a physical healing or some other such positive manifestation which springs from belief. So it's good to have an understanding of how belief operates, and how thought creates within your everyday experience of 'reality'. However, most of the beliefs we hold can be of an unfavourable nature, and can also be a hindrance to our lives, so why wouldn't we want to look beyond them to discover something which is *real* and of a genuine and lasting quality?

Our Reality is always there, resting patiently outside the spectrum of thought, belief and philosophy. Therefore you have to be bold enough to peek out from under all of this thought in order to live in Reality. I hope that you are brave enough to consider the notion, that spiritual awakening has nothing whatsoever to do with religion, philosophy, belief systems or spiritual rules and regulations. There's no prayers, incantations, funny sitting positions, mudras, mantras, recitations, hypnotic suggestions, past life regressions or uncomfortable postures required, to gain insight or acquire first-hand knowledge into your true Reality as the Oneness with all of life. Awakening is about gaining true freedom and realizing *experientially* what you are. It's about first hand familiarity with your true Reality as Spirit.

Now, the truth is that those seemingly 'innocent' philosophies and belief systems of the world have been responsible for much of the world's hatred, fighting, carnage and destruction. *Still* to this day we can see it going on, with people fighting over religious belief systems. Even those who subscribe to a non-dual philosophy can be found to get into philosophical heady debates, which at times border on having arguments. It's that old *"I'm right and you're wrong"* mentality which religion has plagued the world with for so long. Not until the world awakens from this thought programming which it is so spellbound by, will the world awaken to find Truth and lasting peace.

Being born again:

When we hit upon the end of the spiritual search, it is really only like a beginning. For when the search ends, then the finding should follow soon. It's a bit like being born again, or being renewed into a new life. Even though the outer life may remain the same, everything is as if new, vibrant and injected with life, seen as if for the first time. Awakening is a rebirth and a rousing from slumber, as we step out of dreamland and are born again into the *Real* world of Oneness.

Many think that when the spiritual search ends, then that is the conclusion of all the wonder, thrills and adventure which the search sometimes brings. But when the search ends, it is only then at that point that the *real* adventure can begin. At that point, when we recognize that we are no longer interested in the merry go round of seeking, it is then that we may finally allow the awakening within our awareness of Spirit. Then we would find that all of the merriment which the spiritual search has brought us in the past, pales in comparison with this great adventure which awaits us, as we turn away from seeking and move in the direction of finding. For at this point, we will find true wisdom growing steadily within us. We will see things as they really are, and we will be liberated from the maze of thought, and all of the lies we once believed in so deeply.

However, once you recognize that you are no longer caught up in the merry go round of seeking, and you notice that you are tired of the search, well then, that is when you may drift into a kind of limbo state for a little while. Depending upon your willingness to allow the awakening to occur, this limbo state will be as short or as long as you allow it to be. It is like a purgatorial state, lying in wait between seeking and finding for those who lack 100% readiness to _surrender_ into the now, and be metaphorically born again. During this time you may have all of your spiritual assumptions and beliefs totally destroyed, as you progressively move away from mere belief towards the desire for what is real.

If you are not 100% ready to align your attention with the present, then you run the risk of slipping into a depressive mode, as your false perception of Reality gets untangled and dissolved. It is here that we begin to recognize, that everything which we have believed about ourselves, and all of the meaning we have had in our lives, was held together in our mind like a tapestry made of thought. Really, it's all absolutely nothing but meagre thought. In other words, our whole sense of 'me' is nothing but a psychological conglomeration of thought swirling around our awareness and none of it is _real_ at all. To many folks, the undoing of this mental phantom can be hard to take.

Perhaps most of this undoing will have already occurred as a result of your search, but really, it will only be as difficult or as long, as the strength of your desire to hold onto the un-real. Everyone is different when it comes to the willingness of allowing awakening within ourselves. It can be a painful thing to let go of everything we have built up in our mind, which supports and tells the continuous tale of 'me'. But a sincere seeker of Truth will not mind letting go of all that is un-real in order to awaken. They will also not mind letting go of the familiar spiritual search they have become so accustomed to.

Those who hold a strong desire for the realization of Truth will tend to let go of everything that stands against them. Those who are still caught up in the egos materialistic world, seeking for retail therapy, chasing after gurus and other outer things in an attempt to make themselves feel better, generally do not even *want* to let go of that which is false. These are the type of seekers who want to believe that there are a great many sacrifices to be made before one can awaken to Reality. They may not realize, that the realization of Truth does not require for one to be making any sacrifices at all, except for the relinquishment of the ego.

Now, relinquishing the ego is hardly a sacrifice, because the ego is not *real*, it is only a gathering of thought in our mind. Therefore we cannot say that we are really sacrificing anything at all. The ego is the sole source of all our fears, emptiness, unhappiness, stress and just about every form of delusion we suffer from. Who in their right mind would not want to let go of something which is nothing more than a heavy burden? It is the ego which has us in depression, it is the ego which has us running to therapy, it is the ego which has us addicted to retail therapy, drugs and alcoholism etc.

Dare we let go of this thought made entity, in order to be spiritually born again? When we trade in the ego for the Spirit instead, then we have made the most sensible and profitable transaction we will ever make. Imagine being able to trade in your trash for something which is priceless. Can you even begin to envision what being spiritually born anew would be like? The great release of tension, the feeling of Oneness and the light and care-free outlook on life, really does feel like a completely new start in life. Now, don't get me wrong here; after awakening you aren't going to be running around with a silly big grin upon your face, buzzing like a cocaine addict. Awakening is really only a simple and casual return to full <u>sanity</u>. It's remarkable when it first dawns, but it's still very ordinary and yet strangely familiar. It's much like returning home, where you really always were, but you were just too busy allowing your awareness to be entertained with thought to realize it.

When you do realize that here and now you are all that you'll ever be, and that Reality is _now_ and at no other time, then you can finally allow yourself to rouse from sleep. Then there is crystal clear clarity in all that you see. You are really _there_, 100% alive, maybe for the first time ever. You are looking around you and it's like you have no edges, like you are space, just empty space. You know that you are nothing, yet everything, and your essence is in everything, yet you also remain as yourself (strange paradox, I know). Words can't really be used to adequately express this. This realization however will fluctuate in your awareness throughout the day. So don't be seeking for some static blissful state, because it isn't like that.

Yes, there's internal peace, even if you have to deal with a 'bad' situation. Yes, you'll feel happily contented, because you are free of the thought spell, which was the only real source of your discontentment. Yes, you will come to know 'yourself' as being that One indivisible unity which is prevalent throughout all existence. However, attention to the present moment (Attentive Presence), being the key to this realization, is very simple indeed. There are no spiritual qualifications needed for something as simple as presence, is there? There's no spiritual search required for you to be as you are, here in the now, presently, fully alive in the moment, is there?

Now, why would anyone want to keep awakening at bay, just so they can hold onto the familiarity of a thought made sense of 'me', which is totally unreal anyway? Why would anyone want to repeatedly saturate their awareness with philosophy after philosophy and belief after belief, talking all the time about what it might be like to know the Spirit, whenever they can directly know it for themselves, right here, right now?

9

The Spiritual Sideshow

Tangential Issues:

As a Truth seeker, one comes across many fascinating topics of interest. Possibly you might have already encountered some of these topics of fascination. However, if you are what the long term seekers call a 'beginner', then what I am about to cover here may help you to recognize some of the traps which befall most innocent seekers of the simple Truth. If you are interested in spiritual awakening, then a lot of the sideshow topics which emerge from the spiritual scene, will only ever serve to pull you off your simple and straightforward course. They will have you philosophizing and heading down many winding tangential roads for years. Some of these subjects include Reiki, Tai Chi, Yoga, Chakra balancing, Shamanism, positive thinking, psychic development and Aura reading etc – just to name a few.

Now, if you are a teacher of one these subjects just mentioned, *hold on* one moment, don't throw this book in the bin just yet. I would agree that some of these subjects do indeed have a lot of benefits to them. But here I am writing about spiritual awakening, which I have come to discover is quite a simple thing. This simplicity does not require a person, who may be solely interested in awakening to get involved with a whole host of side-line topics and issues. If they want to learn about positive thinking, Reiki or Yoga, well then so be it. But I have found that these spiritual sideshow issues have the enormous power to distract a sincere seeker away from the whole simplicity inherent in awakening, and to lead them down a road of sideshow issues, probably forever!

Once we actually awaken to Reality, well then we may find that some of these subjects don't hold our interest anymore anyway, unless of course we want to use them for personal physical reasons or for helping others. I got very interested in Hatha Yoga during my seeking days, because I thought it would aid in my awakening. I was wrong about that. However, I still use Hatha Yoga today because I like the way that it makes me feel and for the physical benefits it provides. Nonetheless, I cannot see how that particular system could in anyway be of use, to one seriously interested in awakening to the truth of Reality.

Learning how thought has a tendency to create in our reality, is possibly the only sideshow subject that would be of any real use to one interested in awakening. This is because, in order to stay awakened from the thought hypnosis we have ourselves under, we need to have an understanding, and indeed, a first-hand experience of how the thought dramas we hold alter and shape our experience of reality. Because due to the type of thoughts which we saturate our awareness with, we can create a make believe heaven or hell experience for ourselves. If we realize that we are doing this to ourselves with our very own thinking, then we may finally be ready and willing to do something definitive about it.

Knowing first hand, that we are creating our experience of life with our own thinking, helps us to realize that we need to either improve upon our thinking, which is a bit of a sledgehammer approach, or we need to let go of our thoughts altogether and totally shift into actual Reality instead, which is a whole lot easier than trying to 'improve' our thinking.

Now, if we have the tendency to create a happy hypnosis within our mind, then I feel that we will be content with our experience of life just the way that it currently is, and will therefore be less likely to opt for a shift into Actual Reality. But however, if we have been creating hell in our mind, then I do

113

indeed feel that we will desperately want to let go of our hellish thoughts as quickly as possible, in order to discover the promised peace of Reality instead.

One, who is experiencing life as a living hell should be more likely and willing, to permanently put an end to all thought dramas (including force fed positive ones). Actual Reality, I feel, would be more enticing to this type of person, who will most likely have reached that point, when they have had enough of the effort and stress of trying to become a 'better' person. This is why they would be more likely drawn to the cessation of effort and 'becoming', which is what awakening is all about. It is certainly not about substituting your gloomy thoughts with make believe – which is of course, what positive thinking is all about.

Of course, since you are reading this book, I am assuming that _authentic_ awakening is what you are really interested in. If developing a new thought identity as *'Joe the spiritual seeker'*, or if swapping around tired and miserable old defunct thoughts for new 'better' thoughts (positive thinking) is your game, then this book isn't for you, that is a point I honestly have to make. This book is pointing at spiritual awakening (Reality), not the substitute game of making a 'new' ego for oneself.

All that improving your mind-set stuff is still within the domain of a thought induced unreality. Yes to be sure, it is still a more preferable and enticing unreality to be playing about with thought in this manner (changing negative thoughts to positive thoughts), rather than to leave your mental processes to pure chance, where your conditioned mind-set and the world about you dictates how your personal reality is going to be experienced. It is a noble undertaking, but it is still a reconstructed make believe – a happy hypnosis. It is a sideshow pursuit that has its benefits, like most of the spiritual sideshow topics a stereotype Truth seeker will encounter, but having said that, it has nothing to do with awakening to Reality.

Positive thinking is a bit like pasting a thin veneer of positivity over whatever trash we may have lying in our mind.

Soon cracks will appear in the veneer of 'positivity' and you will realize that the old thought system is still there, lurking beneath the glue of the 'new me'. Then you have to go to the bother of continuously applying a lot of effort, just to maintain the illusion of the happy positive 'new me'.

I finally came to an understanding, that the pasting on of a false positivity didn't correspond with actual Reality, and that all I really had to do, was to find what was truly real within me and then I would be okay, since you cannot improve upon the absolute Truth. Engaging ones attention with actual Reality is a totally different ball game from positive thinking. Aligning ones attention with Reality is natural whenever we ignore all of the side issues that we come upon, whilst we are taking a ride on the spiritual seeking rollercoaster.

Whilst we remain hypnotized in day dreams by our chattering mind, with its positive or negative thoughts and the rollercoaster emotions which emanate from those thoughts, we will always need entertainment to keep us sedated or buzzed. Thought needs interesting stuff to get its teeth into and chew upon. This entertainment takes many forms of course, but it all has just one purpose - to keep some semblance of 'meaning' in the life of the hypnotized entity, who unknowingly has become a prisoner to their very own thought processes. There is of course a whole array of 'spiritual' subjects and interests for the mind made 'me' to relieve its boredom, frustration and hollowness with. All of these activities give the thought entity ('me') a sense of purpose. It keeps the hypnotic effect of thought constantly churning within our awareness, as the mind mulls over every subject we encounter which appears to be from a 'spiritual' source.

Now, as awakening dawns within the awareness, we will realize that the only *real* purpose of this world is to regain our natural state of sanity. All other supposed 'purposes' are only things that we do. Until we let go of our thought created divisions and insanities, we will never regain our natural state of sanity. Thought is the cause of all this insanity. So, are we going to forever be slaves to thought? This is why even the apparently 'progressive' practices of the 'spiritual' sideshow, can be a waste of time to one who is seriously interested in matters of the Truth. Since a serious seeker of the Truth, will surely soon come to the understanding that the 'spiritual' sideshow, including positive thinking, is just another deceptively alluring tributary upon the rollercoaster of thought drama.

Food for Thought:

I recall that the spiritual sideshow gave me a new lease of life, excitement and wonder when I first bit my teeth upon its hook. My thoughts finally had some 'good' quality 'spiritual' food to digest; and digest that spiritual sideshow food they did voraciously.   The dream of the 'new me', Keith Loy, the stereotype Truth seeker, took over where the old miserable defunct thought system left off. I then had more pressing issues to deal with, rather than sit around whinging all day about 'poor me'. I had all of my new exciting spiritual knowledge to make sense out of. The new spiritual 'me' I was weaving in my mind, temporarily made the world appear to be a nicer place, more mysterious and enchanting.

I had to 'become' a better version of what went before. I tried so desperately to paste positive thoughts into my mind, because all of the books said that was what I had to do, in order to 'become' a 'spiritual' person. I was so very sincere in my search for Truth that I refused to believe that any teacher would be filling me with a head load of confusion. I needed to believe those teachers, because if I didn't believe them, what would I do and where would I turn? I couldn't go back to the darkness that haunted me, before I learned of the spiritual life.

A lot of teachers fertilize these paths of sideshow interest at every step. They will always highlight how hard it supposedly is to 'attain' awakening. Of course, this belief will then send someone who so desperately needs to awaken to Reality, into a head spin of intellectual concepts, beliefs and second hand opinions – food for thought. If it is food for thought we require (boredom relief) then look no further than spirituality, because it could keep your thoughts entertained and fattened up for the rest of your natural life. And the sad fact is, that is exactly what happens to most of us Truth seekers.

We start out hearing about spiritual awakening (enlightenment) and we begin searching for it, maybe to escape from a depressing life situation. We claim to want awakening above all else and we say we want to know the reality of our true nature, but when we latch our thoughts onto the weird and wonderful aspects of spirituality (the spiritual sideshow), we can so very often completely lose our way in an ocean of beliefs and second hand 'spiritual' theories. Spiritual knowledge in itself is not the problem. Proper spiritual knowledge could be of help, since we first need someone to point the way to Reality, in order for us to ever discover its Truth.

The problem is with our focusing exclusively on spiritual knowledge, without ever applying what we have learned from that knowledge. We run from one book, seminar or guru to another as quickly as we can, without ever allowing what each book/guru is saying to actually sink into our awareness and be applied in our lives. In this regard, we collect a whole lot of knowledge from many different sources, which will all end up being a mish mash of contradiction. Each teacher will be administering their own particular prescription for enlightenment. Each teacher's methods will vary. Sometimes the methods employed vary a great deal from guru to guru. This leaves the gurus contradicting each other. This contradiction we encounter from guru to guru, will most definitely confuse us if we are someone who spends our valuable time running around after each new teacher that arrives on the scene. This kind of searching leaves us lost, in a maze of conceptual and tangential issues – food for thought.

I met a man once, who used to be an alcoholic and once suffered from depression. This man told me that he read Eckhart Tolles' book 'The Power of Now'. That book, he said, was the only book he ever read on the subject of awakening. What was the result of him reading that one book? Well the result was that he actually awakened to his true nature. That was the result of him reading <u>one</u> book about awakening. I asked if he ever read any other books, even minutely related to spirituality, and he answered with a definitive *"No!"* His own words were, *"Why do I need to read any more books or see any gurus? That one book awakened me to my true nature. I used what I read in that book to awaken out of depression and also alcoholism. Now I live only from my true nature and no longer from thought. So why would I need any more books or teachers, other than that one book?"*

Good point – Don't you think?

Lost in a Spiritual Dream:

We end up getting lost in the thought dream of spirituality, all of those side issues which I refer to as the spiritual sideshow. If we don't pull our attention away from those side issues, we will remain within the hypnotic grasp of thought, mesmerized by the happy hypnosis of the spiritual sideshow forever without ever having awakened to Reality.

So what exactly does this spiritual sideshow consist of? What is it exactly? Well, to give you an idea, I will recount from my own life experience how I wasted over ten years with this distracting sideshow. Like I said earlier, I was a voracious reader of spiritual books, so much so that every part of my being got weighed down in the accumulation of second hand conceptual knowledge. This theory distracted me from awakening to Reality, but I didn't leave it there, I had other distractions.

One of my teachers convinced me that it was important to see auras, so I spent a lot of time on that. I was told that I had to feel the energy circulating around my body, so more time was spent on that. I also had to make of myself a spiritual

118

stereotypical 'new me'. Now that definitely gobbled up a lot of my precious time. I practiced a whole host of meditation techniques. I studied Yoga in its entirety which led to my becoming a Yoga teacher, which then caused me to study everything a stereotype Yoga teacher was supposed to know about. I thought that to impress my students I would need to learn as much as possible about auras, chakras, Reiki, Psycho Synthesis, spiritual healing, Tai Chi, anatomy and physiology etc. Now I studied all of that so I could become an all knowing and 'wise' Yoga teacher; but of course it was all just an extreme distraction (a sideshow), away from the real issue that I actually wanted from all of this spiritual stuff in the first place, and that was simple awakening.

I would read spiritual books first thing in the morning, and then again after work. Amongst the reading, I would be practicing a heavy schedule of meditation and energy exercise techniques. I had so many practices to do, that I eventually had to use a timetable to fit it all in. I also found myself distracted by other strange topics that the spiritual scene spawns, like UFOs and lost ancient civilisations (Atlantis myths being my favourite). I gave every moment to this stuff. I now know that I surely must've bored people stiff during this time, ranting on in their ears with all of my new strange beliefs. I could go on for a few pages more here with details of the distracting subjects I studied, but I won't, it tires me to recall it all, and I'm sure it would tire you to read about it.

This spiritual sideshow engrossment consumed my life. It fed me a large assortment of thought dreams, which ate up my life, year after year after year. I loved to talk about it all the time. When I finally did manage to get others all wrapped up in it, we would spend hours discussing, hypothesizing, arguing, disagreeing and agreeing and then of course we would try to recruit others into our uncanny ways of thinking.

The spiritual sideshow left my mind hypnotized with opinions, concepts and beliefs. I became convinced that I knew the answers to all maladies. Although, all of that knowledge was of no real use when it came to awakening, except the simple teachings which were pointing the way to the plain Truth all along. But during this time, I largely overlooked these simple, uncluttered teachings, finding them very philosophical and nice, but I had this insatiable inclination to 'know' more. My greedy all-consuming appetite for more spiritual knowledge, considered it necessary to pig out and get fat on the spiritual sideshow.

It is because of the entertainment which is gained from the 'spiritual' sideshow, which makes it all so deceptively captivating. It does indeed make the dream of the false 'me' more bearable. Unfortunately, it also keeps that dream alive. We add the spiritual sideshow onto our false and fragile sense of 'me' and attempt to make all of that 'spiritual' stuff a part of what we are. This is where we may feel the need to turn ourselves into a spiritual stereotype. Where once upon a time we might have said to people when meeting them, *"Hello there, my name is Bob and I'm a mechanic; I like the colour blue, my drink is Jack Daniels and I also love action films"*. Now since we may be caught in the dream of trying to become a 'spiritual' person, we might instead say upon meeting others something like, *"Hi my name used to be Bob but now I'm called Flower Child. I used to be a mechanic but now I'm a spiritual seeker. I like to keep myself poor because I hear that 'God' hates rich men and look at me now. I walk real slow and I talk real nice and polite, if you smack me on the face, well, I'll probably let you break my arm also."*

Now, if we only stopped trying to be 'spiritual' and allowed ourselves to be real, we would find that we already are this spiritual being we are desperately trying to turn ourselves into. So good news, you already are what you seek. The only reason why you may not know it, is because your awareness is currently crammed with thoughts. Yes, just thoughts. Thoughts of who we are, thoughts of who we have to become, thoughts of how we hope the world is viewing us, thoughts of belief, thoughts of opinion, thoughts of outdoing others, on and on and on it goes. Yet at the base of this mental distraction, is the following belief - *I'm not good enough, so I therefore have to improve 'me'.*

That belief is what has us accepting, that we are not worthy of spiritual awakening. It makes us feel that there is something intrinsically wrong with us, even if we are genuinely nice people. It is that belief we hold, that keeps the self help teachers in business. Maybe some of the genuine teachers we meet will tell us that we *are* good enough, but will we listen to them? Do we really believe them? So, hopefully now you will see that you don't have to become a so called 'spiritual' person anymore. You don't have to hug trees anymore, eat vegetarian food or burn incense in order to awaken to the Truth that sets us free. Just let all of that thought distraction go. Leave your awareness attentive to life as it is, and the Spirit that you are will fill your awareness with its essence.

How long must this go on?

How many gurus are we going to have to study the writings of? How many teachers are we going to follow? How many years are we going to waste trying to fake a smile, attempting to 'become' a spiritual stereotype? You can't fake Spirit you know, because you are Spirit. You are already the Reality which you seek. Let us all now awaken from the games of the spiritual sideshow, all of those little moments of intellectual spiritual head games. Here we all are, tending to the branches of the tree and we ignore the roots. What happens to the tree when the root is neglected? It withers away and dies, therefore producing no fruit. Are we going to let our zest for Reality wither away and die, producing no fruit, just because we are too busy tending to the branches of the spiritual sideshow?

Do you want to let awakening slip through your fingers, just so you can conceptualize all the days of your life, with a smarty pants play of words and an endless flow of philosophies? If we truly want to realize that pure and simple spiritual Reality, that freedom that is our true nature, then we have no choice but to let the conceptual head games go for good.

My thoughts had me believing that I was not good enough to awaken. I thought only special people awakened and that it would not be possible for me to wake up until next year, or maybe the year after that. I'd wait around until I got my holidays off from work and I would intend on using those holidays to practice real hard to wake up. *Sweet Jehovah!* The amount of holiday time I wasted sitting in my bedroom staring at a wall, hoping to have a spiritual high. I would love to go back in time and hit myself in the face with a spade. How hypnotized I was. It was always tomorrow when awakening would happen, because I had more divergent issues to deal with, like the alluring branches of the spiritual sideshow.

If I felt tired, I would postpone awakening to another day, as I thought awakening couldn't happen when I was tired. Another of the funny beliefs I had, was that if I used slang language or swear words, then some mysterious force or 'God' would deliberately withhold awakening from me. I thought that so called 'bad' words would act like a barrier to my realization of Truth. As daft as it sounds, I used to expect my wise guys to be spiritual stereotypes who wouldn't curse or use slang words. I remember I had this teacher during my seeking days, and he uttered an 'unholy' obscenity whilst speaking with me once, and I can assure you that I was none too pleased with him, that's for sure. Of course this was when I was lost in the thought dream, of becoming a spiritual stereotype.

Seriously though, what has the utterance of a word got to do with waking up? What has it got to do with anything in Reality? I suppose if your life is all about moulding your behaviour, to becoming a slave to the spiritual stereotype, well then language is a really big deal for you, isn't it? Well, at least it is a big deal for your hypnotized and learned false sense of 'me' anyway - lost in dreams of becoming.

We need to be honest with ourselves if we are to ever awaken from our hypnosis. This slave to the spiritual stereotype is more sideshow antics. It is just another delay tactic, emanating from the egos own version of spirituality - seek and do not find. With my awareness saturated with the many rules and regulations of 'becoming' a spiritual stereotype, I'm surprised I ever shook it all off. However, spirit will never accept a stereotype as its chosen expression, for stereotypes are thought constructs, they are unreal fictitious entities. Spirit will express itself through the awakened exactly as they are. This true spiritual expression will automatically make right what hypnotic thought made appear as being wrong, because only thought can be wrong in its attempts of self-renewal

These attempts of self-renewal are just another dream, another lie. These are attempts at altering what has already been made perfectly. We only require the awakening within our awareness of that perfection, which is already there. These thoughts of making a 'new me' cloak that perfection and tamper with it, leaving us more lost in the hypnotism of thought as a result. In Reality there never is a 'new me'. Awareness may be hypnotized by a grouping of apparent 'nice' thoughts for a little while, but these thoughts are vulnerable and they require constant maintenance in order to be kept in place. Reality requires no improvement at all. We require only a little shift to Attentive Presence. This takes us out of the dreamland that is hypnotized thought, and unifies our awareness once again with the One true Reality, exactly as it is.

10

The Egos Spirituality

Spiritual entertainment:

I was always curious as to why we feel the need to become part of a spiritual group in our endeavour to wake up to Reality. Surely awakening is an inner matter, which only we are responsible for allowing within our awareness? The lingering belief is that if we are part of a spiritual group, or if we sit in what has been called a 'satsang' session it is going to make awakening easier for us. However, this is completely untrue, since it is only up to you and you alone whether or not you awaken to Reality.

Many believe that sitting in the company of a realized teacher will help with our awakening. Though, nobody can awaken you just because you are sitting in their presence. This doesn't even make sense. Some teachers can help you to have momentary energetic spiritual experiences, but these will fade after you leave the company of the teacher. After you leave the company of your spiritual group or teacher, you will find that awakening is indeed all up to you after-all. If you are being entertained by the thought dramas which you persistently allow your awareness to be saturated in, then it does not matter how many gurus you visit, or how many sessions you have sitting with a spiritual group; you won't awaken, because you don't *really* want to awaken. Who wants to awaken to Reality when they are having an entertaining dream?

I was part of a few spiritual groups in my time, and I never met one person within those groups who was fully awake. I was told by these groups, that if I joined them it was going to make awakening simpler for me, but these groups only helped me veer completely off my simple course of awakening to Reality. Everyone would sit around bouncing beliefs and concepts off one another, and there were spiritual sideshow interests and many contradictory prescriptions for enlightenment being discussed. The contradictions that were being aired within the groups would leave the mind boggled with confusion. I can tell you, that if you were focused on the simplicity of awakening and then joined one of these sideshow groups, your understanding of simplicity would go straight out the window in a haze of mystification.

But what is the real reason for our joining a spiritual group in the first place, I wonder? Is it really because we think they will help us, like a support group with our awakening? Or is it possible that we use them as part of a spiritual entertainment? If entertainment is the reason why we join these groups, then entertaining they certainly can be. Sideshow spiritual groups can also help to reinforce whatever spiritual beliefs one has adopted. It sure seems to be the case that birds of a feather do indeed flock together. If we hang out with others who carry similar beliefs to our own, then our beliefs will be further reinforced, won't they? Buddhists will be drawn to Buddhist gatherings and those from, let's say the T.M. movement, will be drawn to others within that movement. This however, all works the same way as did the old religious systems, *"Oh good, you're one of us"* some might say.

Nevertheless, beliefs also have nothing to do with awakening whatsoever, since you could be a complete atheist and still awaken to Reality. The beliefs that most of us carry, most likely could actually be based on, well, based on nothing but belief really, because we may not have any actual experiential evidence of what it is we claim to believe in. If our beliefs were based on true experience, then they would no longer be beliefs, but they would rather be based on absolute certainties.

Say for example that you believe in chakras. Well, do you have any evidence in your own experience of that, or do you merely harbour a belief that a guru or other source passed onto you? Now you may love to think that the guru is telling you the truth; maybe even the guru believes that what he is saying is the truth also, so you unquestioningly believe what he says. Then you may argue with folks who disagree with your second hand hypotheses. But don't you see that these beliefs are within the domain of thought, and are therefore not Reality? They can therefore have a hypnotic effect upon our awareness.

Honestly consider the following questions. What do you believe yourself to be? What do you think it is that you are? Are you conforming to a stereotype, because you believe that is what you have to be, or that is what you are? Look within yourself and truthfully appraise this question - Could what you believe about yourself, just be some thoughts and memories mixed together in your mind, to cast a spell of 'me' upon your awareness. What are you really?

Do you believe for example, that you have to become a spiritual stereotype, in order to be good enough for awakening? Do you believe that there is a man in the sky who is going to look down upon you, and dish out awakening as a present for towing the line of a strict 'spiritual' path? Have you, your family, your society, your guru or your spiritual group hypnotized your awareness into thinking that you are a certain type of person, with certain fears, with certain complexes, with a concrete personality?

You may enjoy your beliefs, like a good entertainment, and they may give you comfort, just like any good thought will do, but beliefs can actually hold us back from awakening to Reality, since I have observed that many believe awakening to be an elite and special state of being. A lot of people and spiritual groups believe awakening to be a super human state of mind, reserved only for the guru and not for them. The belief in it being an extremely difficult thing to accomplish, would also keep one searching for this state forever, thereby projecting it eternally into the future. This belief will act as a block to awakening, and so also will the belief that one is unworthy of awakening. These beliefs cause a hypnosis upon our awareness, so much so that we don't even question them.

Indeed beliefs of any kind are just hypnosis in disguise, since they are not a living Reality, but are merely thought constructs. Beliefs, I finally came to understand, were nothing more than hypnotic thought swirling around my sleeping mind. I realized that beliefs were of no use, when you want to wake up from the hypnotic dream of thought. The spiritual groups I was a part of certainly had their rigid beliefs. One of the beliefs was that our group was the _only_ group with *thee* answer to spiritual awakening. The let's pretend teacher who hosted the group, would talk about people who were not a part of our group as if they were the poor lost sheep. Our mission of course, was to go out and recruit as many people as we could to join us, so that they too could be 'in with the in crowd'.

It is strange of my group holding this belief, that we were the only ones with the answers, whenever back at this time nobody within the group was actually awakened. The self-styled guru we had at the front of the room, well, she done her best to convince herself and us that she was 'the real deal', as one of our group members referred to her as. But it's sad you know, I deep down knew back then that she was very much not awake at all, but I refused to acknowledge this to myself for a long time, since I thought I needed the group in order to 'achieve' awakening. However the group was once again just another front, another platform for promoting the egos spirituality.

The Spiritual Competition:

I will try to avoid using the term 'cult' as much as I can here, but a lot of these spiritual group meetings we see taking place everywhere these days, are indeed like cult clans. Maybe if you reading this have a group of spiritual minded friends, well maybe your group are an honest bunch of real nice people; maybe they're genuine, and do their best to help each other along the way. If you are all genuinely interested in awakening and interested in awakening alone, well then maybe your group will be of some inspiration to you.

However there are groups out there who are not Real nice people at all, but fake nice people. These are the cult clans I refer to. The main focus within these cult clans is not spiritual awakening, but tends to be more upon getting new recruits and outdoing each other 'spiritually'. These groups tend to be breeding grounds for spiritual stereotypes.

At a meeting of a cult clan everyone is usually sitting around in a dimly lit room, looking mysterious, eyeballing each other, with some trying to smile bigger than the guy sitting beside them. Someone is sure to kick-start a spiritual competition. This involves everyone comparing spiritual experiences. Some will be trying to outdo everybody else with their strange spiritual experiences. An exaggerated version of this would be something like the following.

"Heh Jack, I seen yer mans aura the other day, really bright and big it was!"

"Did you see that Nelly? That's super, you are really coming on now, aren't you? Of course I saw a few orbs myself the other day and yer mans aura also"

Then from away off in the corner of the room, a man stands up trying to conceal his envy with a manic grin, as he hollers across the floor,

"Huh, Is that all you experienced? I saw orbs, auras, UFOs, ghosts and I seen into another dimension twice, oh yeah!"

Here we have the egos out-do mentality at play, *"I'm more spiritual than you are"*. This is the unconscious quote of the egos spiritual competition. I nearly prefer the 'my car is bigger than yours' mentality, than this so called 'spiritual' version. But this is all a part of the spiritual competition, we got to feel like we are on the ones on top, don't we? It takes the edge of the inferior feelings that arise from being stuck in unreality. Take it from one who has traversed this road; be very careful when your intention is to awaken to Reality. The momentum of the ego can take your pure intention, and pollute it with anything to keep you asleep.

The ego will create 'spiritual' thought dramas just as readily as it will create any other type of thought drama. I feel that most of us will continue to create these mental dramas, until we get sick sore and tired of drama in its entirety. Even when everything is going well, I've noticed that some of us (not all), tend to make mountains out of mole hills. Why? Well because the drama fascinates us and relieves the boredom that might be our everyday lives. It gives our mind something to chew upon.

A question for you - Does drama (including 'spiritual' thought dramas) give your mind something 'nice' to chew upon? Do you honestly want to let go of your mental dramas in preference of Reality?

Even many 'spiritual' teachers are afflicted with the 'spiritual' competition, and the egos need to be seen as being the 'special' one. If he or she happens to have a very charismatic personality, then they will find many seekers lavishing the reverential treatment upon them which they desire. Some of these teachers have quite a good business going. The closer their followers get to the simplicity of awakening, the more confusing the teachings become. After all, if we awaken easily from our sleep, then our 'spiritual' teacher is out of business.

Many seekers also believe that we need a teacher to sanctify our awakening, or possibly to give us a certificate of recognition. Without a teacher to tell us, how would we know if we were awakened? Now, do I even need to ask this question? Would we really need someone to clarify it for us? Would we need someone to say, *"Well done, you are now awakened, congratulations, you've finally made it as a high ranking member of the spiritual hierarchy. Here is your certificate of awakening. Would you like it framed?"*

Or maybe our certifier would negate our awakening, bursting our eager bubble by remarking, *"Sorry buddy, I'm afraid you haven't made it this time. You've got a lot more years of meditation and listening to guys like me ahead of you before you can 'become' what you already are".*

Also, many teachers make awakening appear to be a very strange state of being, granted only to the selected few. A lot of the do 'nothing' teachers contradict themselves a lot, because half an hour after telling you to do 'nothing', they will then be giving you a way to 'do' this nothing, which will sound very much like *being in the now.* But they will tell you that what they are talking about is not *being in the now,* because there is no now, and even if there was, there's 'nobody' there to be in the now anyway. Also, amongst teachers there is ndless on-going confusion as to whether or not being present is doing nothing, or if it is doing something, or whether one can even 'do' it at all.

I have even heard some teachers of nonduality say things like, *"depression and pain is okay, since that is just 'what is' and it happens to 'nobody' anyway".* Obviously teachers like this have never suffered from depression themselves, or they wouldn't be making ridiculous remarks like this. Then, due to your confusion concerning this nonsense, they will say, *"your confusion is also 'what is', and so it doesn't matter whether you understand or not".* They will also tell you that if you don't understand, then not to worry, because there is a mystery within you which does understand.

Unfortunately, it is not that mystery which needs to understand, since that mystery is eternally free anyway, but your awareness is not free, so your awareness does actually need to understand, and it does need a good clear pointer. Now, a spiritual teacher is meant to give this good clear pointer. But heh, if they don't give you that good clear pointer, don't worry about it. Apparently it's alright to be confused, but just make sure you don't forget to pay these teachers for their 'service' on your way out of the room, and be sure to bring a jar of ointment with you to their satsang, so you can rub it onto that cut you've scratched into your head, because scratch your head is all you will ever be doing in the presence of these guys.

Philosophy of this nature seems to be about as much use to the seeker of Truth, as algebra is to a one year old baby. All of that talk leaves the seeker many years down the line, caught with a head full of contradictory philosophy without having actually awakened. Oh well, maybe if we don't awaken in this 'life' we can awaken in our 'next' life instead, huh?

So, you can see that some teachers would not be very helpful to one lost in confusion and in search of Reality. We should not be so naïve, in thinking that surely all spiritual teachers would have our best interests at heart. Proceed with caution would be my advice to you, though try not to be cynical, but make sure you are also not naïve. Don't forget that these teachers are meant to aid you in your awakening; they are not there to confuse the issue further, or to be worshipped. Maintain absolute trust in your own intuition and you shouldn't go far wrong.

Now, I'm not saying in all of this that we should shun the guru, but quite the opposite. I am suggesting that we possibly for the first time *actually* listen to our teacher for a change. What is he/she saying? Is he/she a truly helpful teacher? Don't you realize that an authentic teacher won't want you following them around year after year? No truly helpful teacher wants an eternal student. That would be a bad reflection upon him/her as a teacher. If you ask an authentic teacher, *"what do I have to do to awaken to Reality"* they will speak back to you quite directly and straightforwardly, occasionally using a metaphor or two to convey the inexpressible. Then again, maybe it is you who are failing your guru, rather than him/her failing you. Maybe you love the spiritual sideshow too much to be bothered with awakening to Reality.

Before *my* teacher would talk to an audience he would joke around, but he always had a serious meaning behind the jokes. He would say things like - *"Here I go again, who am I speaking to today, the deaf or the dead? Is this just another meeting of the more people? You are always after the more, yet here I am and I'm just going to sing the same old song, until who knows, maybe someday, somebody actually decides to listen."*

Then one day it dawned upon me that I was one of the 'more' people he referred to – one of the deaf and the dead. I had heard my teacher make this statement many times, but I always figured that he was talking about some others in the audience, and certainly not me. When I realized that he *was* actually talking about me, it was somewhat humbling. This led me to take a good look within and to finally get real where awakening was concerned. All of those years I wasted with the spiritual sideshow and the egos spirituality makes me now shake my head in disbelief. All of those years spent searching, chasing and reading whilst Reality was staring me in the face all along.

For the sake of our Reality let us no longer consider awakening to be a special state, belonging solely to gurus. Let us no longer drape that Truth in mysticism, shrouded in weirdness and held at distance by cult clans, whose only interest is entertaining themselves with the spiritual sideshow and its offshoot, the egos spirituality of seek and do not find. This is what our religions have been spawned from, hence the confusion and divisions inherent within religion. As a result, religion has caused more strife than anything else upon this planet, even unto the present time.

Let us not waste any more of our own time. Let us accept graciously the aid of those pure and simple authentic awakened teachers, but to take that direction they give us and produce fruit with it, rather than more shackles which only bind us to those teachers of Truth. We may corrode the sincerity of even those simple and pure teachers, with our needy aspirations of being someone's eternal disciple. In this endeavour of chasing down teachers to follow, we will never find what the real teachers so desperately want us to find.

11

Refining Reality

The now is always now:

Surely once we define the target of whatever it is we are seeking for, it is then only a means of discovering the quickest and most simplistic route, to the attainment of the desired result. After all, these days we have an enormous supply of books and gurus out there apparently pointing the way, leaving it then up to us to apply what we hear or not. But this enormous supply of teachers and books can become a part of the problem.

Too much choice can confuse us, especially when the choices between this path and that method are oftentimes contradictory, to say the least. One guru says to 'do nothing' to attain awakening, yet another tells us that it is an arduous path of effort and self-control. I guess it would be a little confusing for example, if we were driving our car and needed to get to a particular destination; then we came upon a crossroads on our journey, only to discover that there were a lot of road signs all pointing in different directions, yet claiming to be pointing the correct way to our destination. Which road would we choose? Which road sign would we trust? Maybe all of the road signs do indeed lead to the same destination, with some taking us 'there' quicker and easier than the others.

However, could it be the case that most seekers don't actually know, what it is they are really searching for? For example, if a Truth seeker was asked, *"Why are you doing all of that meditating and reading all of those spiritual books?"* The

134

most likely and probably popular reply would be, *"Well, I'd like to be enlightened"*. Now, if we pursued the question further with, *"Enlightenment, what's that?"* Then assuredly, we would be hit with a whole array of differing opinions on what enlightenment is. There would be contradictory translations and confusing explanations galore, defining that one word, 'enlightenment'.

To be honest, I haven't got a clue what people mean anymore when they use the word enlightenment, because everyone seems to be confused about what it is. Even the gurus give different translations on it. I feel that it is a word we could do away with, because then it wouldn't confuse seekers anymore, about what it is they are actually searching for.

Some would consider enlightenment to be a super human state, only reserved for those like Jesus, Buddha, Krishna, the 'saints', the ancient Yogis and gurus etc. Others would clarify it as the natural state of the human being, and certainly not a super human state at all. A lot of folks would tantalize us with poetic sounding interpretations like - *"Enlightenment is the state of transcendental, unbounded, super conscious, all pervading and omnipotent oneness with the All that is, the Absolute I Am that I Am, the infinite and ever present one life from which all life sprang forth"*.

On and on it would go, each one giving his or her own view, and maybe they would even be arguing over who held the correct view. Just like most of the world religions have been doing since time began. Seekers might tell you that enlightenment was their goal. Some would claim that it can be realized immediately; whilst others declare that it happens over many lifetimes of incarnation. Who to believe? Who to follow? Who is right? I imagine you would be left like I was for some time; eyes wide open, jaw drooping down, bewildered, confused and scratching your head murmuring *"What the hell?"*

However, the Spirit is already there, within us and within everything that is all around us, indeed we are the One that appears as 'everything'. So how difficult can it really be, to wake up in awareness of what is already the case, that which is the Truth of our being?

ANSWER
As difficult as we believe it to be, or want it to be

Now why would we want it to be difficult to awaken to our true nature? Well, let me explain. I have heard many wise folks say stuff like, *"It's not about reaching the destination; It's the journey that makes life so worthwhile"*. Well, that to me is very true about this journey of life, here on Earth, in which we tackle goals to achieve our life's ambitions. It's fun as we set out to achieve each goal. However, it is not a wise statement, when it is applied to waking up to Reality, simply because Reality is always here and now, that's why. The realization of Spirit does not require one to embark upon a journey and that's the whole point. How can you journey to something that is there, right where you stand? Reality is also not a destination, because the word destination implies that what you are seeking for is somewhere else, and that it is not present here and now within you. The now is always _now_, it is not in the future and that's the whole point.

Therefore, we adopt the rather ridiculous belief that we have to make a 'journey', to where we already are, so we can arrive at a 'destination' in which we already reside. We would realize that this so called 'destination' is already the case, if we ever cleared our awareness of the thoughts we have it filled with. Now, I feel that we have applied that wise statement I mentioned, not only to our goals and ambitions, but to our desire for Reality as well. Therefore we have made finding Reality a future goal to be attained, and boy are we going to make sure that we enjoy the so called 'journey' to it, with all of our sideshow distractions leading us down thrilling, yet long and winding rickety roads.

It's the thrill of the chase, as huntsmen would say about hunting a fox. Huntsmen don't really enjoy the capture of a fox.

What they enjoy is spending the day tracking the fox. Then when they catch sight of the fox, the adrenaline rushes through them, as they chase after the poor little fox. When they catch the fox, they have to start all over again, because they are not satisfied with capturing the fox, so they start out upon another hunt. They are only thrilled with hunting and tracking, don't you see?

Do you get it yet? What do most seekers of Truth do? We spend all of our time hunting and tracking after Truth, and when the way to Truth is finally staring us right in the face, we ignore its simplicity and set out upon another time wasting hunt.

The End of the Rainbow:

It never worked too well during my seeking days, believing that awakening was a future goal to be attained, requiring years of meditation and study. Awakening was in my mind, and I feel in most other seekers minds, as being akin to the crock of gold at the end of the rainbow - mysterious, distant, enchanting, yet forever out of reach. This belief led me on a wild goose chase for years. Sadly what did I expect, when I set the natural state, as a future goal? A lot of seekers don't accept the awakened state as being the natural state, since their assumption may be that if it was natural, then surely we would already be aware of it. Now that's a good point for one to be making. But then one wouldn't have to hypothesize very much, to see why we are not aware of our natural state.

We are born into the world and we are very much aware of Reality to varying degrees as small children. Maybe you can remember the magical feelings you had as a small child. The world had a crystal clear clarity and wonder in it that seemed almost Heaven like. But the way that our cultures and education systems are set up, with the effect of conditioning and conformity; it allows for our natural Attentive Presence to be drowned in heavy dead thought. We then learn to grow the unnatural habit, of letting our awareness sleep in thought dreams and dramas. We do this because it is what we see everyone else doing, so we do the same thing. That is why gradually throughout our childhood; we find that the magic of life fades away, until we end up later on down the line as sleepwalking adults, lost in a maze of thought dramas.

The first thing I noticed when I finally allowed myself to wake up, was this magical feeling arising again in my awareness; that magical perception I had once known long ago as a very small child. It felt like I had gone to sleep somewhere along the line, and now I was only waking up, wondering to myself where the hell my life had gone to. I felt like Rip Van Winkle, the guy who slept for years and missed out on real life. I actually realized that throughout all of those years I had spent as a sleepwalker, I wasn't really *there* at all. I couldn't even really say that I was alive throughout those years. I now see those years as time I had spent living like a zombie, as I was thoroughly possessed by an entity called ego.

However, the realization of Spirit is always readily available; it is not lying at the end of the rainbow. Yet, in my mind (once upon a time) awakening was forever at the end of that rainbow. I would always be thinking of getting my greedy little spiritual claws on enlightenment, and thereafter I would be a 'special' person who could be like none other than Jesus or the Buddha themselves. When I actually awakened, I realized that none of us are special. We are all equals, whether we are awake to Reality or asleep in thought dramas, it doesn't matter.

Awakening is simple at the end of the day. It only depends upon whether or not we *really* want it or not. It has to be our number one *priority* in life, simply because it is a 24-7 thing, which we carry into all avenues of our life. In this, we have to be honest with ourselves. Are we really seeking awakening or are we just philosophers? Do we treat the teachings of the awakened like a hobby to pass our time away, or do we truly seek for clear direction within those teachings? Let's refine our search for Truth, for only then are we likely to find what it is we are seeking for. To those who do awaken, one thing is always realized - that when all is said and done, awakening is easy after-all.

This simplicity of awakening could be described in terms of a still pond. If we stir up the water of the pond, the mud from the bottom rises and makes the pond look clouded, dirty and unclear. No reflection will be seen clearly on the surface of that pond, as long the water is stirred up. How do we make the water clear again, so it is able to hold a reflection? We leave the water alone and stop stirring it up. This allows the mud to settle back naturally and effortlessly to the bottom of the pond, thereby leaving the pond clear again to hold a reflection.

Similarly, if we lack Attentive Presence and stir up our mind with thought, our mind will become clouded, dirty, unclear and unable to perceive Reality. When we leave our mind alone and no longer stir it up with thought dramas, we notice the mud (thought) effortlessly settling back to the bottom of the pond (our mind) all on its own; and our mind is clear again, being able to reflect Reality upon its surface.

As we apply lots of effort in our desire for Reality, rushing around from guru to guru and book to book, frantically searching for Truth, we end up standing in our own way as a barrier to that Truth. We stir up our mind with the mud of conceptual thought. We seek for Spirit like a hypnotized person does for that which was always the case. Then we believe that the One is lying at the end of a rainbow, forever out of reach. Yet we are already the One, which is driving the engines of the body, lending power to our thought construction, the dream appearance that we mistake as being who we are – that which we call 'me'. The sunlight of Spirit is always shining away within us, in all its brilliance. It is just the clouded murkiness of thought that obscures its light from reaching our awareness.

When I allowed my awareness to clear and settle, I noticed that this feeling realization was something familiar to me. It felt like I was returning home, after being away for a very long time on an over-extended journey. I understood then, that my tiresome efforts at trying to 'become' better and thinking that I could make 'me' spiritually perfect through effort acted as blocks to awakening. That notion of, if I only practiced a few more spiritual disciplines or maybe if I did go to see that new teacher of Advaita, or take a month off work to sit on a mountain top, all would be better, maybe then I'd 'get' to be enlightened. The delusional thought in my mind, which produced these pursuits, packed its bags reluctantly. However I had truly reached the end of my tether with it, and was glad and very much willing to usher it out the door eternally.

I now realize that Spirit is our natural state, inherent within us all, nothing supernatural or super anything about it. It's just the Truth and it's what we are. It's Truth devoid of lies (hypnotic thought dramas). It is Reality devoid of the thought made little 'me'. It is awareness freed to the Spirit in an extremely casual yet careful manner.

Why need we be careful? Well this world is full of people caught up in the thought spell, so we must take care not to let the dramas which emanate from other folks hypnosis infringe upon our awareness of Truth. Nobody is a Superman and I feel we could all get a little too smart for our own good, when it comes to maintaining the realization of Spirit. We must remain on patrol, on guard against the false thought processes which may be coming from ourselves primarily, but also from our hypnotized friends and associates, who remain willing to stay asleep within the dramas of thought entertainment.

If we find ourselves momentarily unawares, then these dramas which others project upon us, could drag us back into the egos boring and tiny world very easily. If these dramas are being projected from others towards you hard and heavy, then you'll find that you are not a 'super' being after-all. You might actually have to leave certain people in your life behind, if they continuously project dire thought dramas towards you. Unfortunately, that's just the way it is if you want awakening to be a lasting realization.

We need to get real with ourselves, and define once and for all, what it is we are actually seeking for. Is it a little peace of mind? Is it spiritual entertainment? Is it philosophical knowledge so we can sound impressive to our friends? Perhaps spirituality is an ego thing for us, in order to erect ourselves upon a podium, above the rest of humanity, so we can look down upon our equals, yet not wishing to see them as equals. What is it, we may ask ourselves that has taken us to the path of spirituality? Do we want realization of the simple Truth (Reality)? Now, that's the big question, isn't it?

12

The Natural State

A small switch of attention:

A few years into my spiritual search, I travelled from Ireland to visit a spiritual teacher in California. I paid this teacher rather handsomely with a five figure sum of money. I was naïve enough to believe that he would send me back home to Ireland forever enlightened. When I did return to Ireland, sure enough, I found myself in a bit of a high state, but it was a happy hypnosis of positivity I was experiencing rather than anything which emanated from the Spirit.

I couldn't wait to tell everyone about how great this teacher was. I repeated his teachings verbatim to everyone I met. I visited my sister Annette one afternoon shortly after returning home from California, and I shared with her what I found to be the most interesting aspect of this teachers methods, which was that small shift of attention called 'being in the now'. Of course, I didn't think that she would pay much attention to what I was saying, since she was not at all interested in spiritual matters back then. She had no background in spiritual matters at all in fact, but surprisingly, she did listen to me. She even promised that she would 'practice' being in the now, although I didn't think she actually would, since many people hear all about living in the present and never proceed beyond the philosophy of it afterwards.

So, a few days after talking with me, Annette rang me one night on the phone and related the following message to me.

She said - "*You'll never guess what happened. I'm not even sure myself. I was practicing being in the now tonight and I started laughing and couldn't stop. I was tingling all over, like electricity running up and down my legs, hands and into my head too. So I kept practicing it and I felt like, I don't know how to put it, like I wasn't there anymore, like I was everywhere yet nowhere, it's weird. I don't know how to explain it. You're going to think I'm crazy when you hear this, but I was looking around the living room and it was as if I was everything, everything was me, everything was alive, like everything in the living room was aware of me. Then I felt like I had slipped into an emptiness, but at the same time, it wasn't an emptiness. Am I going nuts? What the hell happened? You never said that would happen to me. It freaked me out so much, I had to go and turn the telly on to get back to normal. I'm still buzzing with this electrical energy stuff*".

Now, I was rather shocked by this message which she related to me. I didn't think this could happen to someone with no spiritual background. How could this be? She had simply sat down in her living room and switched her attention from thought to the Present, with this awakening as a result. I always figured that one would have to do a lot of relaxation and meditation as a prerequisite to awakening, but it seemed that this wasn't the case after all. Most spiritual seekers have usually heard all about awakening from books and gurus before it occurs, so when it does happen it isn't that big of a shock, or at least the shock is minimized due to the understanding gained beforehand. Annette hadn't got that background, so I spent the next half hour on the phone explaining the nature of what had happened to her, from my own limited perspective at that time.

After that night of transcendence she had caught the spiritual bug. She would relate spiritual experiences she would be having to me on a regular basis. For years afterwards we would engage in many longwinded conversations about spirituality. However, we both unfortunately ended up complicating it all for ourselves with the spiritual sideshow. For a further six years, despite our having come upon the definitive answer to awakening, we would veer completely off course and deep into the spiritual sideshow issues, away from the simplicity of that original and simple switch of attention from thought to Reality.

With the best of intentions I gave Annette many books on spirituality, and it was due to the confusion and contradiction inherent within these many books that the simplicity of presence, which she had already found, had been contaminated for her. It was around this time that she stopped relating spiritual experiences to me. The happy hypnosis of the spiritual sideshow dampened and darkened the perception of simple Reality for both of us. This spiritual sideshow contaminated something which was so simple for Annette, something which she had found instantaneously. However like myself, she has come full circle again, shaking off the spiritual sideshow, and at the time of this writing she is once again conveying the simplicity of awakening.

I have since learned that the ego loves to take hold of a spiritual experience and conceptualize it to the death, so that it remains only a temporary experience and is never allowed to grow into a full spiritual awakening. The experience is then turned into the egos own brand of spirituality - seek and do not find. This is when the ego strikes an unconscious compromise, offering us the happy hypnosis of the spiritual sideshow instead of a full spiritual awakening, which would then certainly bring about the egos demise.

The experience my sister had the night she spoke to me on the telephone, I could've explained simply what was happening to her, and then just left it at that. From deepening and integrating the experience, she would have found her own inner guidance and then learned all she needed to know about what was occurring within her. This would have been first-hand knowledge, not second hand, like what is gained from books and gurus. She would then have had no need to follow any spiritual sideshow issues. These issues only serve to leave us drifting for a while in a happy hypnosis, instead of awakening to Reality. All of those spiritual books and various teachers, I now know contaminated the simplicity of awakening for both Annette and myself. Afterwards, we both fell into the trap of *believing* that being present was a very hard thing to do, without one having to hide away from the world. The same belief is what many others worldwide have held for millennia, and many spiritual seekers still unfortunately hold it today.

In fact, I have found that most seekers these days become very defensive when someone tells them that awakening is easy and natural, whenever we really and honestly want it above all else. It's almost as if they love the happy hypnosis of the egos spirituality far too much, even more than they would love awakening to the Real thing. They tend to react to one who is telling them this, as if one is pulling at the foundations of their world. Which of course, in a subtle kind of way, one actually is.

I found my experience with Annette to be an excellent kind of science experiment. Annette had the same experience that a lot of the gurus out there have been reporting. Indeed it seems that many seekers worldwide have been seeking for most of their lives and have never come upon this experience of transcendence before. So why did someone like my sister, with no spiritual background or previous interest in any sort of spiritual matters, hit upon this kind of transcendental spiritual experience on her first attempt at simply being present? It's peculiar, is it not?

We are good enough:

So, why do I tell you this story about my sister anyway? Well for example, does it not state quite clearly that awakening is easy, effortless and natural whenever it is approached without the contamination of endless concepts and spiritual theories? Does it not state, that our conceptualization of awakening does indeed infect its simplicity? I believe it also brings to a close that there are no prerequisite fires of purification, self-improvement, self-discipline or any of that sideshow stuff necessary after all. We do not need to change our name to something that sounds mystical, nor do we need to walk around moving slowly and speaking softly, with a falsely generated half-baked smirk upon our faces.

This story makes the declaration that we are good enough. Right here, right now, just as we are, we can move into that Reality of the Spirit. We merely need to pay attention to the simple diamond at the heart of all spirituality, and indeed all true spiritual teachings. We need to ignore all of the sideshow trappings, which are aimed at diverting our course away from full spiritual awakening. All of those philosophical concepts are a deceptively tricky and sly entertainment (food for thought). It is food for the false mind made 'me' to get its teeth into, in order to keep its survival intact. That mind made 'me' leads us into a grouping of day dreams which tire our minds and bodies, draining us of life force, and sadly we have come to accept this state of affairs as being 'normal'.

Now, if I can sit down with my sister Annette, and give her information that opened the doors of her perception immediately, thus enabling her to experience the Spirit that she is, with no background knowledge on her part; well then, do we really need this constant chasing around after gurus, and all of those countless spiritual books? I think not!

"Aaahh," you might be saying, *"but she is only one case, maybe it's not that easy for all of us."* Well then, according to your faith let it be done unto you. For what you believe will happen will nearly always be the case. Could it be that our belief in *'hard'* is the reason for the never ending search? Maybe so, it seems to me. By the way, Annette was not some kind of natural spiritual stereotype. She got stressed at times, she enjoyed her wine at weekends and funny enough, she was also a meat eater. So, she didn't naturally adhere to any spiritual stereotype behaviour patterns. Nothing needed to change within her to produce awakening, except for a small shift in her attention away from thought into the moment.

The qualities of the Spirit are all good, so when we allow the expression of Spirit in our awareness, we find that we reactivate our natural character, not a stereotype. Through awakening we find that the natural characteristics we have are like a vehicle which the Spirit will use in order to engage in this world. It is the hypnotic dream of thought identity (egoic 'me') which awareness shakes off through awakening. We simply do not take this illusion seriously anymore. Yet we can still enjoy the natural characteristics.

Today, this moment, you could make the unequivocal decision to drop thought dramas from your mind and shift into Attentive Presence. You'll find that thought has a certain momentum to it, but like anything which has momentum to it, if it is not being fuelled and propelled with our constant attention, that momentum will surely slow down with the new momentum of awakening taking over. I would suggest that you don't complicate it all for yourself, but simply reduce all of the spiritual teachings you have heard down to this one thing – Attentive Presence! Seriously, this is all that is required in order to awaken to Reality. Attentive Presence undoes all that is not true, and all that is not really you. All of those thoughts which come together to create within your mind a falsity of 'me' are what you allow to be undone. This permits the real you to come alive finally within your awareness.

Now, Attentive Presence cannot strictly be called an exercise or a technique; it is rather a mode of being, of which we seem to have two. Attentive Presence is the mode we shift into for the expression of life (Spirit) as it is, in its purity. This mode leaves us awakened and free in Reality, liberated from the prison of hypnotic thought, awakened to the unity of life (The One), at ease, in peace, contentment and joy. The other mode is the mode of being we know all too well, and that is the mode of the sleepwalker. This is the mode where the average person goes around like one who is still asleep, lost in daydreams and trapped in the hypnotic daymare of a thought induced unreality. Which mode do you choose? I know which one I choose.

Maybe now you will see that awakening doesn't take time, only a true willingness to allow it to happen. If any part of awakening takes time it is only the adjustment period, when we are getting used to the new yet strangely familiar awareness and clarity of Reality. We may for a little while drift back and forth between Reality and thought, as we allow the growth of this new habit, this new focus of our attention. Yet this period is as short or as long as our desire to leave behind dreamland and the self-imposed character of fiction (ego) - the thought constructed 'me'.

We have spent so long, being caught up in the spell of thought that we need to be careful during this interim period. It may for a time seem like everything and everyone we meet is coercing us to slip back into our old thought dramas. Don't think of yourself as being the invincible one when this happens, because we can all too easily slip right back, under the influence of the hypnotic spell of thought at this juncture. However, when I finally hit this point, I found it natural to shift my attention from thought to Reality, since I didn't particularly like my thoughts anymore; they were no longer much of an entertainment.

I then recalled all of the true wise gurus I had read about, who stated how easy and effortless it was to awaken to the Truth. Although beforehand, I never really believed what they had said. I now however finally grasped what they meant. I just wasn't ready to let go of the mental effort back then. Reality is a persistent caller however and has a tendency, to knock on the door of one's life all the louder whenever the Spirit is being ignored. The spiritual sideshow burned me out, and it wasn't until then that I heard the call of the Spirit (Reality) loudly, very loudly. I finally did away with all of the complexity. Yes, all effort to 'become' I turned my back on. I pulled myself from the residue left over after the fallout of the egos spirituality. I then allowed myself to awaken, this time without interfering or conceptualizing about it all. As a result of making that simple switch of attention - that simple non-action - I awakened casually and effortlessly to the One Reality that I am, and the natural state of order I am forever immersed in.

13

We're Not Worthy

Freedom or slavery:

I would like to ask that you pause for a few minutes before you continue reading. For your own benefit, please take a moment to consider an honest answer to the following question.

What do you really want - Freedom or slavery?

I know, at first glance it appears to be a pretty weird kind of question to be asking, doesn't it? Surely the answer seems obvious. Or is the answer really as obvious as it appears, I wonder? For example, do you see yourself as being a slave to thought? If you do see yourself as being a slave to thought, then you must hold a *belief* that you are a victim of your mind. Or maybe you feel that you are unworthy of awakening. If that is how you feel, then you are subscribing to a form of slavery, which will be kept in place as long as your feelings of unworthiness persist. Deception breeds even more deception. When you feel unworthy and believe in that unworthiness, then your feelings of unworthiness will grow stronger; it's a vicious circle. That is, until you break the pattern of course, and then become arrogant enough to say, *"I am ready to be the master of my mind!"*

Awakening isn't a game that you can play with, and it isn't something for the bored and the restless to entertain themselves with. Victimhood and beliefs in unworthiness have

150

no place within an awakened mind. Your victim mentality has to be put out with the trash if you really desire to live in Reality. So, getting back to the question I asked - well, do you want freedom or slavery? Have you honestly considered what your answer is? Have you even considered the implications of your answer?

Your answer, providing it is a true answer and not one thrown out by the ego, is going to provide real clarity to establish if you are actually *ready* for awakening or not. The only prelude which is necessary for awakening to occur is whether or not your readiness is in place. It has nothing whatsoever to do with how many gurus you have visited or how many 'spiritual' books you have read. It has no relationship with how many koans you can unravel, or how well you can recite sutras or various spiritual discourses. You could have been a spiritual seeker for many, many years and may still not be willing to move beyond philosophy and the daydreaming mind in order to enter your Reality. On the other hand, you could be an alcoholic or a drug addict, and this could be the very first book you have ever read on the subject of spiritual awakening, and your readiness and willingness could be 100% perfectly in place.

We tend to think that just because one has been meditating every day for twenty years that makes them a perfect candidate for awakening. But this is not the case at all. The best candidate for awakening is one who has reached the end of their tether with the internal fantasy land of thought. It is when you grow somewhat weary of the content within your mind that you tend to look elsewhere for a better way. Have you ever had a bad day and found yourself thinking, *"There's got to be a better way"*.

Readiness is based upon how much you <u>want</u> that better way. It is also based upon how much you desire peace. You might not have ever meditated in your life, but if your readiness to make that small shift of attention from thought to Reality is absolute, well then, you might awaken whilst an ardent meditator may not. So an honest answer to that question, of whether you want freedom or slavery, is going to set the foundation for whether or not awakening is ever going to happen for you. Until you make a firm internal shift or decision, between Reality and fantasy, or freedom and slavery, then all you can really hope for is a few momentary spiritual experiences every once in a while.

Abiding realization comes from that powerful decision to opt for Reality over your daydreaming mind. That decision helps us to see through the charade that is the thought world. When we see through the charade, we tend not to take it seriously anymore, and therefore, it no longer has any impact upon our perception. When we make that firm decision, based upon a knowing internal feeling that we have reached the end of the line where the ego is concerned, then and only then, can we see the light at the end of the tunnel we have been living in.

Your answer to the question I have asked is the choice between fantasy and Reality, ego or Spirit and the Truth or mere philosophy. It is the decision to awaken to your true nature, or to remain asleep in daydreams. However it must be emphasized that the decision cannot be made with the thinking mind (ego), but it is more a _certainty of feeling_ which comes to you, when you know for sure that you are finally ready to move out of dreamland and into the now of life, just as it is.

Now, unless we choose freedom, then we really are like willing slaves; slaves to the mechanical thought process which we willingly allow to contaminate our pure awareness. Now, I assume that everyone who reads this will most likely jump in with the answer, *"Yes, I want freedom!"* But I wonder, do you really? As a Truth seeker, do you really want to let go of the willing slavery? How much of your daydreaming mind are you ready and willing to let go of? Are you ready to take a bungee jump into the unknown? How much do you value the prospects of absolute freedom?

Well I guess the answer all depends upon whether we like the egos pain, stress and discontentment, or whether we prefer the Spirits peace, happiness and inner fulfilment. Seems like a pretty straightforward choice, doesn't it? We might assume that surely everyone wants peace, happiness and inner fulfilment, but take a look at some people and see how they appear to get a kick out of upsetting themselves and everyone else around them. I have observed that some people will always opt for a stressed frame of mind full of trash thoughts. I don't know, maybe it makes an otherwise uneventful life appear to be a little less boring.

Some folks also like to indulge in feeling unworthy of the Spirit, as they perpetually play the role of the victim. Even when all is going well in life, these types will search for something to rock the boat. So it may be unwise of us to assume that surely everyone would choose freedom over slavery. Even a lot of Truth seekers want to hang onto a victim mentality, rather than take responsibility for their own awareness. Many prefer to derive their familiar sense of 'me' from the habitual discontentment of their perceived heavy 'past'. The heavy 'past' of course, is just nothing more than thought dramas rattling around within their mind, but try telling some of them that. It's like trying to take an unwilling junkie off their heroin. If the junkie doesn't 100% really _want_ to get off the heroin, then in the long run, it isn't going to happen. It's exactly the same for the Truth seeker. If you don't _totally_ desire the freedom of spiritual awakening over your thought dramas, then in the long run, it also isn't going to happen.

Like the puppet on a string, most of us are at the mercy of, and are subject to, the pull of hypnotic thought dramas which we might _refuse_ to even question the so called 'reality' of. We might refuse to question these inner dramas, simply because we find them to be so damned entertaining; like something major is always going down with 'me' and my 'life'. Through awakening, it becomes quite evident that nothing major is ever going down. It's all just thought dramas playing tricks in your awareness, creating the soap opera you call 'my life'.

So the answer to the question, of whether we want freedom or slavery is an important one. It allows for us to get *real* with ourselves, possibly for the first time. When we finally get real with ourselves, and establish within our mind whether we actually do want to let go of our victimhood, or whether we want peace rather than stress, Reality over fantasy, or the Truth over a mere philosophy; it is only then that the way can finally be cleared for spiritual take-off (so to speak).

Beyond belief:

Do you feel unworthy of the Spirit and union with the One? Many folk do, simply because most of us were brought up in a religion, which led us to believe that we were all a bunch of 'sinners'. I recall at the age of seven; I and my fellow class mates at school, were told by our teacher that we were all natural born 'sinners', so none of us could ever claim to be 'good'. Even at the age of seven, I recognized this as being a whole lot of old rubbish, so I naturally didn't accept it. However, I recall that most of the other boys in the class *did* accept it at this time. We were asked by the teacher to stand up in front of the class if we considered ourselves to be 'good'. So at this young age, I was the only one in the class who was 'arrogant' enough to stand up and tell the teacher, *"Heh, I am good"*. But the teacher rather angrily told me that I had better sit back down again very quickly or 'else' – so naturally I sat back down again.

I noticed repeatedly throughout my life that a lot of religious people, and indeed many 'new age' Truth seekers, tended to get rather angry when you disagreed with their beliefs of unworthiness. Eventually it became shockingly clear to me, that their beliefs were simply a form of hypnosis. Belief is a mixture of thought and concepts which we take on board without any proof. Now, our beliefs could be erroneous, but we don't even want to consider that, now do we?

Well, let us see; test yourself here and now. Do you find a little irritation arising within you as I say that your beliefs are a form of hypnosis? Don't you realize that the irritation comes from having a fixed opinion about something, which you have allowed to _saturate_ your awareness? You have made that opinion a part of your psychological 'me' (ego), and when that opinion or belief is questioned, you usually feel like you are being personally attacked. However, if our awareness is saturated in any form of thought, then we cannot really claim to be genuinely free. We are a puppet being dangled by the puppet master of thought identity (the ego)!

Now, I'm not asking you to agree with me here, because then you would be caught up in believing again. I am suggesting however, that maybe you try to be brave enough to do a little digging within your own psyche. Perhaps you think that _your_ beliefs are true? Well, where is your proof that they are true? If we had proof, then they would no longer be beliefs. If we had proof they would be certainties, wouldn't they? This type of questioning might be a little frustrating for some, but it does bring great clarity, because when we question the thoughts (beliefs) we hold, then we might actually have a chance of seeing beyond those thoughts, and then discovering actual Reality where the Truth is to be found. Realization of the One is quite literally beyond belief.

Now, religion for example, does a great deal of promoting the idea of spiritual unworthiness throughout the world. We, as simple folk tend to suck this in, and we become somewhat hypnotized by it. At times it seems to me, that we as a species get a secret thrill out of these feelings of lowliness and unworthiness. It is somewhat disconcerting that in today's world, if we even admit that we _love_ ourselves, it is frowned upon. What then, are we supposed to hate ourselves instead?

However, when we realize that it is only our thoughts which create the facade of unworthiness and limitation we appear to hold so dear, what are we going to do about it? Do we enjoy feeling like a victim? Is there really some kind of secret thrill we get out of feeling limited and unworthy of the Spirit? Are we going to continue weaving this tapestry of discord within our mind, or are we going to simply let it go? When we do decide that we want peace, happiness and inner fulfilment, we can simply align our attention with Reality. We can then divert our attention away from the heavy and dead useless baggage of thought we may have been carrying around within, and direct that attention towards life as it is right now.

Upon hearing this, many who claim to want awakening will steadfastly claim that it's not just as simple as that. But you're sure to know deep down that it is as simple as that, but we firstly love to play a little game of cat and mouse, don't we? We enjoy the spiritual search; the game of 'catch me if you can'. It keeps the *we're not worthy* mentality on-going. It keeps the dream going.

Waking up from dreamland is only based upon which seems more agreeable to you; your daydreams or the prospects of awakening to your true spiritual Reality. You only have to be willing to accept that you *are* good enough for this realization. You most certainly *are* worthy of the Spirit, since it is what you *actually* are. It is what's *Real* within you, and the thought dramas you have been fooling yourself with are most certainly not real.

Once you are finally 'arrogant' enough (like me) to accept that you are worthy, then accept this also - it is not hard to pay attention to where you are. It is not hard to fully experience life through each of your senses right now. Is it really that hard to listen to what is happening, here and now? Is it difficult to see, smell, taste or feel? Surely it can't be difficult to divert your attention into one of these senses, is it? It only takes a little willingness for it to happen. It is not difficult, nor does it take any time at all to switch your attention out of the fantasies, and to divert that attention into the present Reality, to experience simple life, with sensory aliveness, just as it is.

We do not need to grow a beard like the gurus do. We do not have to memorize a whole pile of spiritual philosophy, believe anything, wear a white robe or erect a make shift halo around our head. There is no need to speak in a false calm voice, burn incense, construct a sacred alter, erect a statue to a deity or to sit in a certain position to simply live with Attentive Presence.

Due to a misunderstanding, we may feel that we have to become a so called 'special' person to make ourselves worthy of the One. We listen to the gurus words and read spiritual texts, and we may then glean an underlying impression that these teachers are _more_ than what we are. Yet any honest speaker on the subject of awakening will always speak of awakening as being the true natural state of _everyone_.

To pay attention to each unfolding moment and to embrace life fully; who said one needs to be a special person to 'do' that? How special does one have to be to simply appreciate the song of a bird? How mystical do we have to become, in order to fully enjoy a pleasant walk through the park upon a summers evening? What beliefs or spiritual training are necessary, to breathe in deeply and appreciate the crisp air upon a hazy autumn morning? Where is it written that we require special initiation or higher knowledge to merely be what we are, where we are?

Really, it's all as easy as ABC. I challenge anyone to present to me a clear rationale for the difficulty we are supposed to endure in order to be as we are, and simply switch our attention into life, just as it is. There is no spiritual development necessary to merely experience life fully in each and every moment. There is no longwinded or taxing intellectual understanding required, for each of us to embrace the ordinariness of every now. What effort is there in letting go of the defective control stick of thought, which we have been turbulently running our lives with, and to flow with the refined and care free stream of life instead?

Did we not all do that as children? Did we as children not naturally play the game of life the way all games should be played, with fun, light heartedness, ease, in peace and in joy?

When did we stop allowing ourselves to savour life? Why do we want our lives to be a continuous struggle, just so we can fool ourselves into believing that we are 'becoming' something in the eyes of the world? When did we all start beating ourselves up, with all this trash about being 'sinners' and about being unworthy of our natural state? Most of us hand over _all_ of our energy to trash thought dramas and delusional beliefs.

"*Let's drink to world peace,*" many people say. Now, how can world peace ever come about whilst the people of the world have their minds in utter turmoil? The ego keeps rehashing the past, and it doesn't care if the past was hellish as long as it is familiar. Familiarity keeps fear at bay, so in an attempt to block out fear, the ego will always keep the past repeating itself. It will just keep repeating the same old monotonous patterns until we grow weary of it all, and we are then perhaps _finally_ ready to look for that better way, which is the easiest of all ways. So, are you finally ready to accept that better way?

The slavery of dreamland:

Contaminating our everyday conscious awareness is a collection of thought which makes slaves of us all. We willingly march to the repetitive beat of these thoughts; this inner tyrant which has become known throughout the world as the ego. As we march to the egos insidious beat, we suffer the emotions which emanate from the dictates of that inner oppressor. Perhaps those thoughts and emotions will make us feel like we are less than we know we can be. Maybe those dejected feelings will hold in place our belief of unworthiness, and our inner conviction that we are not good enough for realization of our true spiritual nature. Recalling from my own life, a time when I was afflicted with this slavery; I can now safely say that I would rather disintegrate into oblivion than to go back to filling my mind with this kind of garbage thought. We fill our minds with darkness and then we seriously wonder why we cannot find a light within the world. Is it any wonder we feel unworthy of the Spirit?

I guess that some folks don't really want to give up the inner thought demons anyway, since the inner demons of thought can sometimes make life seem a bit like a ride upon a fairground ghost train. Yes to be sure, the ghost train can be scary and stressful but it's also exciting. I theorize that it's only when we spend too much time upon the ghost train, and the demons get a tad overpowering and out of hand, that we might *finally* bring about a state of zero tolerance. We may then become very much opposed to the pain these inner demons are causing us. I feel it is only at that time, when we will really want to let these thoughts go, and opt for the better way instead.

But we are so used to playing the heavily rehearsed fictional character we have been superimposing over our true nature, we are hypnotized with the thoughts emanating from it. We are also so identified with the human body as being what we are, that the Truth appears hidden from us. Yet the Truth is not hidden; this is a lie! The Truth is always there, within us and all around us, and we only have to shake off the lies, and then pay attention to the Truth instead for this realization to hit home. What we place our attention upon grows within our life, and what we take our attention away from, dies within our life. Now, when I say pay <u>attention</u> to the Truth, that's exactly what I mean. I don't mean to read a lot of philosophy, in an attempt at trying to figure out the Truth of Reality with our thinking mind. The Truth of Reality stands way beyond anything the thinking mind could ever conjure up. The Truth of Reality can only be lived and experienced – *not thought about.*

Philosophy is just like any other hobby in the world, it can be extremely enjoyable tearing Reality apart and stripping it down into segments with endless ideas and concepts. But we have to go beyond thought, in order to discover that which thought cannot touch. Thought is based upon what we know, it is divisive and it names and labels everything, thereby turning a natural unity into a seeming duality. Even to be speaking of the true nature of Reality is to cut it up into pieces, since words have to be used to describe it. Since language is just more thought, well then, we cannot accurately use language to describe that which is beyond what language has the ability to express. I cannot even accurately express the realization of Truth here within this book, since the realization of Truth is experiential in its nature. All we can really do concerning the expression of Truth realization is to try using language to the best of our ability, to inspire others who may want the realization of Truth to occur within their own awareness.

Yet, once the simplicity of awakening is recognized, we must lay aside philosophizing, because this will only serve to distract us from moving naturally into that present spiritual Reality. The persistent study of gurus' writings, the constant search for techniques and the relentless reciting of second hand wisdom, all merely serve to make that which is the simplest of all attainments, appear as being the most difficult of all attainments. And when it seems difficult, well then, I suppose the endearing thought *'We're not worthy'* will persist forever. Then we will add that belief onto our thought made sense of 'me', and thereby we will be keeping the dream alive forever. Now, do you want to keep this dream alive forever?

We dream up fantasy situations and inner worlds within our mind, which correspond to nothing that is real. In the thought world that is dreamland, we can repeat over and over, again and again, all of our favourite annoyances, our fears, our grudges, our regrets, our inferiorities, our angers, our philosophies and, *oh yeah,* let's not forget our good times too. Dreamland is a world we construct within our mind; a world made of thoughts. It is the world we dream up as a replacement for Reality. It is the world as we would either prefer it to be, or the world as we fear it might be. It is the world of our worst fears and secret feelings of inadequacy. We look through our thoughts and out into the world, and all we see is our thoughts colouring everything and everyone we meet. Truly, until we allow ourselves to awaken to Truth, all we will ever see is our own thought projections.

The world masked with thought; it is this which I call dreamland. It is the land of the un-real, the land of the sleepwalker and the land of the ego. It is here in this dream world where we will find all that we believe to be 'me' (the ego) - that unreal fictitious phantom of the imagination. Let this thought world go from our awareness, and then there will finally be some space left for realization of the One to emerge, it's that simple.

14

Taking a Chill Pill

Spiritual practice:

I recall a time when I was studying to become a Yoga teacher; I was struck one day by how serious many of the aspiring Yoga teachers in my class were about their disciplines and practices. To me, Yoga was all about attaining enlightenment, and enlightenment was the be all and end all of life as far as I was concerned, so I too was rather serious when it came to things like Yoga practice and meditation. However, on one particular day in the Yoga class, a light switched on in my mind as I looked about the room at the other wannabe teachers.

We were all gathered together, about fifty of us in all, and we were receiving instruction in a rather uncomfortable breathing practice by a visiting Indian Yogi. Everyone was sitting on the floor cross legged, with straight backs, eyes partially closed and focusing on this uncomfortable breathing practice for what seemed like infinity. I hated some of the breathing practices they taught us in Yoga. A few of them were very useful for relaxation and calming down, but some of them only made my chest feel like a vice grip was crushing it. So despite being told that this particular breathing practice was going to help increase my 'prana' (life-force) and aid in my eventual 'enlightenment', I stopped the practice after about twenty minutes and instead looked around me as everyone else got on with it.

As I sat there, I found myself reflecting on why all of this meditation, breathing and Yoga practice wasn't producing any enlightenment in anyone I knew of. Of course, they always promised that these practices *would* result in eventual enlightenment, but the evidence to back this up was in short supply. In my mind, and in all of the enlightenment teachings I had heard of, enlightenment was said to bring a state of joy, light heartedness, ease and a letting go of all effort to become. But as I gazed around the room, I noticed for the first time, that there were no signs of 'ease' and 'letting go' in evidence amongst the aspiring Yoga teachers I was mingling with. There was a lot of stringent control in evidence, but certainly no joy, ease or letting go.

Around this time, I was even caught up far too much with various practices, philosophies and techniques, and I was way too much involved in trying to control myself to feel any ease or peace within. As I looked around the room, it became clear that all of my fellow students were the same. We were all programmed with our philosophies, our practices and our stereotype 'Yogi' lifestyles far too much, to even dare to let go, take it easy and chill out.

Whilst I was noticing all of this, I wondered for the first time, if maybe I was wasting my time with all of these practices. Spiritual philosophies and their related practices, were leading me to take life way too seriously to leave any room for simple fun. Along with the philosophies came the list of spiritual rules one had to abide by, which seemed to suck all the juice out of life. We aspiring 'Yogis' usually got tangled up in a mess of heady philosophy as we tried to make sense out of life, creation, living and dying, and what God was really all about etc.

Whilst sitting straight backed and cross legged in the Yoga class on that particular day, with an ever increasing discomfort in my lower back, I pondered over all of this. Then I heard one of my Yoga friends sniggering to herself on my right. I looked round and she too had her eyes opened, but with her hands clasped over her mouth as she tried to stifle her laughter.

163

Finally she got 'control' of herself, and so I leaned over and whispered to her, asking what she was laughing at. She responded with, *"My God look at them all, they all look so uptight, why can't they just lighten-up?"*

She was right of course, after all, Yoga was supposed to help people relax, unwind, find inner peace, move more freely and ultimately find spiritual union, which is what the word Yoga points to. But if it was going to produce a deathly serious person who lived their lives by a list of stringent practices, then it was *certainly* not bringing what it promised. I then allowed myself to laugh at my friends' observation, but partly laughing at myself also for being so rigid and controlling.

Now, in Yoga they use the word 'Atman' to refer to the inner Spirit. There was a theory that all of the practices in Yoga were said to unleash or make known this 'Atman' within ones awareness. So my Yoga friend leaned over to me a second time, still sniggering as she passed comment on this Atman theory; she whispered, *"I don't know about you, but there's no sign of my Atman appearing on the scene today, in fact, with all this breathing going on, I think my Atman has left the building"*.

At that we both burst out laughing, much to the dismay of our fellow students and the Indian Yogi we had teaching us. If looks could kill, then we would've both been dead on that particular day. Though, certainly life isn't meant to be stifled with all of these spiritual practices, is it? To uncover our true nature, surely we don't have to practice anything, do we? After all, if it takes a practice to become aware of our natural state, then that naturalness couldn't be said to be very natural, now can it? Well, if it's natural, then it can't take effort or practice to realize it.

I finally noticed that the good old ego enjoys a nice little practice, because practice always means that you won't 'arrive' at your awakening until <u>tomorrow</u>, whenever you become 'good enough'. And of course, to the ego you'll never be good enough for awakening, because to stand up and shout at the world *"Heh, I am good enough"*, is seen as being the height of arrogance in the eyes of the worlds' sleepwalkers. To those who wish to remain asleep, your awakening is seen as being a threat to their dream world, to their little 'me', to their sense of victimhood and to their desire for drama. Your awakening means that humanity is not the lowly species we all like to think we are. It means that we will have to stop blaming others or some 'supernatural' source for all of the problems we supposedly face.

Yes _your_ awakening is seen as a threat, even to many posing as Truth seekers, and that's why we have a multitude of practices to sift through whenever we take to spirituality. Practice always means _future_ and since awakening happens in the here and now, then it cannot possibly take a practice to allow it to happen. You don't have to practice to become aware of your naturalness. Just let yourself be, give up your philosophizing and all of your spiritual manipulation, and all of your endless games of becoming. Why not take a chill pill for a change? Align your attention with the here and now, with your senses alive. Pay attention to life as it is happening right in front of you now. Let your senses savour life; look, listen, feel, taste and smell life – _Now, Now and Now!_

This is certainly no practice. Filling your mind up with trash thought dramas takes practice, it takes work and it is truly damn tiring. But taking your attention out of thought and aligning your attention with the here and now, well, this is natural and this is how we all lived once as very small children, before we allowed our attention to go to sleep in the dream world. Sleeping in the dreams of thought need no longer be the case however. Right now, you could tie up your attention with life, just as it is happening right in front of you, in this and every moment. Snap the spell of thought which locks your attention into a semi dream world, and awaken with Attentive Presence to the ever present Reality which never leaves you.

Getting real:

As the years progressed from my Yoga teaching days, I gradually moved away from all practices. Eventually I gave up on all philosophies and belief systems also. I realized that philosophy and belief systems were only thought, and since I wanted to move *beyond* all thought they were of no use to me anymore. Indeed, they never were of any use to me anyway, since I didn't want spiritual entertainment, I wanted Reality. However, I still remained a little naïve enough to discuss my new and uncompromising desire for Reality with other Truth seekers. This usually upset them. They would then attempt a version of saving my soul, which meant that I would be expected to accept *their* second hand philosophy, guru or beliefs etc.

To this day, I still occasionally come across folk who wish to 'save' my soul. These people think that I'm lost without their gurus, philosophies and beliefs. They are always trying to spiritually educate me. When I mention how simple it is to awaken from the thought trance whenever we _truly_ desire it, I usually get a reaction as if I have blasphemed or committed an atrocious 'sin'. Silly me, sometimes even I momentarily forget how much seekers are addicted to their spiritual practices, philosophies and beliefs, or better put - to thought! *"Oh well"*, I often say to myself, *"I'll leave them in their little dreams, and I'll continue to go on my ease, flowing in every moment with the care-free current of Life"*.

I guess some folks just don't want to look out from under their heavy baggage of belief and philosophy, to dare to consider that maybe awakening is simple after all. But like I said, it's only simple when you truly desire it more than your wandering mind. When that desire and readiness to awaken is firmly in place, then you'll not need the likes of me to tell you what needs letting go of, because when that burning desire to get *real* takes over you, then you'll find aligning your attention with the Reality of the here and now to be a natural thing.

Unfortunately, I have noticed that some people don't want to get real about awakening, until they have practically driven themselves over a precipice into a state of hell mind. And, as startling as it sounds, some folk, when in that state of hell mind, still make excuses and come up with reasons why they can't or won't move beyond it. To my observations, it appears that some people actually *want* to live in a state of hell mind, and they also want everyone else to live with them there.

So, with awakening, I would say that you have to desire it above all else. You have to be ready and willing to let go of your victimhood, and accept responsibility for your own mind. You have to be willing to get *real* with yourself. The strength of your desire is the fuel which will keep you awake. Without that, the best you can hope for is a momentary spiritual experience every now and then. Now, don't think I'm knocking spiritual experiences. Spiritual experiences are nice, and can sometimes be quite powerful, it's certainly better to have them than not to have them, but a fleeting experience is not what awakening is all about, you have to understand this. Once awake, you'll probably not care much about spiritual experiences anymore, even though they do come more frequently. Most of the time there's just a great clarity, and a sense of Oneness with everything you gaze upon. Because of this clarity, as you look at the world, you will feel like you are looking at 'yourself' a lot of the time.

So, awakening is not about gathering lots of beliefs and philosophies. It's not about reading books and chasing gurus. It's not about acting spiritual or being a good guy either. It's about <u>*awakening*</u> out of your thought trance and seeing Reality as it is, and not as you <u>*think*</u> it is. Then you will no longer be a slave to thought. You'll be free of the mental burden which most of humanity falls prey to. You'll know what you *really* are, and will no longer be fooled with what you think you are. You'll live in peaceful freedom, a slave to no one, a slave to no spiritual rules, philosophies, beliefs or gurus. You'll be a Reality man/woman and no longer a sleepwalker. Then you'll be your own master, paddling your own canoe and singing your own merry little song of life.

But come on, you decide; do you *really* want to trade in your thought dramas for Reality? Why not make this moment right <u>now</u> your crunch time for decision? Don't allow yourself to be stuck on a spiritual path any longer, when you could allow awakening to happen today.

It is a pity that many seekers get stuck, simply because they can't focus on Reality alone, or make that decision to opt for awakening only. Many get stuck with a particular philosophy or teacher, leading them to only ever think and talk about awakening as they attend one satsang session after another. However, being glued to a particular philosophy, and indeed guru addiction, can be detrimental to one who is seeking awakening. Indeed, after awakening I became increasingly aware that to many seekers, awakening was all about revering the guru rather than actually taking on board what he was teaching and using it to benefit one's life. After all, a guru is only a teacher and a human being just like any of us, but because we dream up all manner of strange associations about what it means to be awakened, we end up looking upon these gurus as if they are superior to us.

I've heard of many gurus who are regarded as being incarnations of God, but what we don't seem to appreciate is this little fact - <u>*we are all incarnations of God*</u>. Everyone and everything is an incarnation of God. God is not an individual being which is distant and separate from us all. God is the One unified energy field which we are all One with. This Reality is the great Unity, the One nondual crux of all life, of all worlds, of all dimensions and of all Reality. Awakening brings this Truth into ones awareness, and that is the *only* time when you will know this for sure - when you realize it in your own awareness! You may believe or disbelieve it, but your belief or disbelief is meaningless without the realization in your own awareness.

When you allow yourself to realize this <u>*first hand*</u>, then and only then can you really go beyond all belief. Until that moment you may use belief as a comfort mechanism, and heh that's okay, there's no harm in that, just as long as you don't go out and do what many others have done with their comfort mechanisms, like burn someone, start a war or crucify someone who disagrees with you. I have often noticed that some seekers revere their gurus so much, that they will hang pictures of their favourite guru up in the house, and some will even light candles under the picture. It's a guru addiction they have, but most seekers don't see it as an addiction. They cling to the guru like lost little children, wanting someone to hold their hand and say, *"Don't worry, you don't have to take responsibility for your mind, I'll do it all for you"*.

Instead of letting go into the moment with ease, and going with the flow of the Spirit, seekers appear to want *more* control, more practices, more beliefs, more 'becoming', more books, more teachers, more anything at all, just as long as they can continue living in the thought world. Yet most spiritual minded folks will take to spirituality because they want relief from stress, they want to be free from the burden of the egos world, they want peace, happiness and to feel at one with their world and fellow man. But usually they end up even more burdened, whenever they become entangled in a maze of philosophy and new age spiritual practices. They usually wind up losing sight of their original intention to awaken to their true inner spiritual nature, whenever they begin dabbling in the complex world of spiritual seeking.

It takes great control to live your life like this, but awakening involves the _relinquishment of all control,_ and it requires a surrendering to the flow of life into the moment that is now. It requires for you to take a chill pill and let go. So, by burdening the mind with philosophy, beliefs, spiritual rules, practices and endless 'becoming', seekers are unknowingly taking a step in the wrong direction.

Happiness:

Many people will also take to spirituality because they want to find true and lasting happiness. But I wonder do we ever consider the real reason for our lack of happiness in the first place? Let's face it, if we are filling our mind up with thoughts of an upsetting nature, then can we really not understand why we feel despondent? Most of us never equate our own thinking as being the source of our unhappiness.

We run to the guru, because on some level we think that he is going to have a look inside our mind, and then take out all of the trash we have in there for us. The guru is going to patch us up and then we will be nice and 'cured'. We believe that the guru is going to do it all for 'me'. Yet how can the guru keep _your awareness_ clear and present in the moment? Only we can 'do' that; that is our responsibility, not the gurus. We are the ones who willingly fill our minds up with trash thoughts, and no guru anywhere in the world will ever be able to stop us from contaminating our own awareness with downbeat thought scenarios. No book will ever do it for us, no guru will ever do it for us and no spiritual path will ever do it for us, because we have to do this for ourselves. Only we can decide when we have had enough of the thought trash, and then choose Reality and our happiness instead.

All of the choices we make in life appear to be for the sole purpose of enabling us to experience some happiness, aren't they? I mean, isn't that supposed to be the big driving force behind all of our decisions, all of our ambitions and all of our wants in life? To be happy, that's the great big ideal, isn't it? So we find ourselves doing many things in life, which are supposed to facilitate this great ideal of maintaining happiness.

At the time of this writing, Warren Buffett is one of the richest men in the world. During a lecture he once gave, he told his listeners that if they think their happiness will come from having a big house, big car or X amounts of money then they are very much mistaken. He told them that when he earned $10,000 a year, he was just as happy _then_ as he is now that he's amongst the world's richest. He said that happiness is a state of mind, which comes as a result of doing what you like doing and what you are naturally wired for. He said that he always did what he liked doing (which happened to be playing about with the stock market).

Now, here is a man whom many would not consider at all to be a 'spiritual' person in the strictest sense. But upon observation, it's plainly obvious if you studied this man, that he's only happy because of his attitude of mind, and because of his ability to play the game of life like the game it was meant to be. He was never interested in being anybody else other than himself, *just as he is!* He dances his own dance, and sings his own song (so to speak), and he became highly successful in an _unattached_ way as a result of that attitude of mind.

A lot of folks who chase after all of the things they *think* they need to be happy, appear to find that they still remain unfulfilled, despite treading all of the superficial routes which are supposed to bring lasting fulfilment and happiness in life. So, if the superficial routes we tread upon are found to fail in bringing the happiness and fulfilment which they promise, what then is it that we are actually supposed to do in order to bring about and maintain the happiness which we seek? What are we going to do when the superficial, and indeed the materialistic avenues of life have let us down? Are we going to start living our lives in the flow of the moment, doing what we love to do, activating our natural interests and talents and then playing them all like a game, just as someone like Warren Buffett does? Or will we continue to struggle through life, seeking amongst the superficial and materialistic world, believing that material things have the power to enliven us and make us forever happy?

In the attempt to 'make their lives work', even many spiritual seekers struggle with spiritual disciplines and practices to get where they think they want to be. And of course, after all of that struggle they are usually not happy, just rigidly addicted to philosophy and belief; so what was the point of it all we may ask? They spend many years of their lives _practicing_ how not to be happy. Consider that even the Saddam Hussein's of this world, all did what they did because they wanted to be happy. Even if they went about it in some macabre and twisted ways, these people actually think that their struggle will have a glorious and victorious end, which will bring great happiness into their lives.

However, struggle and effort will never lead to happiness, because you will be perpetually denying your present source of inner happiness, by casting your happiness into the future. Only those who embrace their natural self and flow in the moment with the great game of life can truly be happy, and can only accurately be said to be a *real* success in life. Allowing ourselves to be mentally at ease with each new day, no matter what is happening; now that's what *real* success is. When we flow in this manner, then there is no stress and no struggle to get where we think we want to be.

So you see, this is the importance of flowing with the current of life, in the moment, here and now, just being as you are, playing your game the way you are uniquely wired to play it. Sometimes you win and sometimes you lose, but you are unattached either way. That's the beauty of living your life in the moment; you generally don't consider that big 'scary' future which the rest of humanity is always talking about. This leaves us in a happy state; in a peaceful, care-free and naturally relaxed state, and then that opens one up for a spiritual awakening to take place.

15

The Peace of God

The egos world:

God, or as I prefer to call it - *the One*, did not make anything imperfect. Look at the great sophistication of this universe, where everything works in harmony. Look at the complex organism that is the human body and the intricate manner in which it operates and grows. It certainly seems to be the case, that all of nature has its own role to play, in the maintenance of life on earth. We too I'm sure, have our own natural role to play, just as much as the rest of nature has. However we do indeed, appear to be in stark contrast with nature in fulfilling any sort of life giving role to this Earth and its ecosystem.

We seem to be cutting ourselves off from our natural state of Spirit, thereby cutting ourselves off from nature. Now we operate from a destructive mode, a mode of mental sickness, which we mistakenly assume to be sanity. Anyone who is even half awake can see clearly that we as a species are very dis-eased within our mentality. We operate from a mind-set that is not at ease with itself. This mind-set we have come to refer to as the ego. We, somewhere along the line, lost awareness of our true natural state in union with God - the One. Now it appears that we are adrift in the void of space, with no understanding of ourselves, with no apparent purpose, or indeed, no idea if we even had a purpose in the first place. How did this all happen?

Here we are arrogantly claiming to be the rulers of this Earth. We cannot even take care of ourselves, or so it seems, so how can we dare to have the fantasy to say that we control the world. We do this obviously because of a madness that we clearly hold in our minds. This madness has taken the throne in our awareness, where once upon a time the Spirit which is what we truly are, held its enchanting sway.

Why I wonder, did we allow that madness of ego to seize power in our awareness? Going by the crazy history of this world, I guess it all happened so long ago that we now forget how we all ended up like this. We do have theories and beliefs as to what happened, but no true actual account, other than the myths and long held tales, which have been handed down to us from generations long gone by.

When we are born into the world, we find this madness surrounding us, so much so, that we take it as being normal. Due to our blind acceptance of this madness being normal, we as innocent children copy what we see the others doing. Due to our copying what we see others doing, we also end up within this grasp of hypnotic thought (the ego). And so the momentum of ego continues its reign in the world unabated. From generation to generation it gets passed along, from one to the other, like a baton does in a relay race. Those who challenge the reign of ego have been ridiculed, mocked, ostracised and even killed, for having the audacity to firstly awaken themselves to the Truth, and then secondly, even more so, when they dare to embark upon the quest of helping the rest of humanity to awaken from this slumber we are so spellbound by. A truly helpful awakened teacher will always have this ridicule lurking in the background of their lives.

Yet no matter what happened to bring us into this current mode of egoic consciousness, it can now finally be rectified, but only if we are honestly willing to let it be rectified. We don't really need to know how we ended up with this sleepwalker egoic mind-set, trapped in a spell of hypnotic thought. All we truly need to know is firstly, what the problem actually is and then we need to understand how to eliminate the problem. The problem is clear to be seen. We are lost in a hypnotic spell, weaved out of the thoughts we allow to roam through our awareness minute by minute. We are all like sleepwalkers, who stand as if comatose to the present Oneness of Reality, which is the absolute true nature of life.

The very nature of the egoic mentality is inferior, and many get caught up in seeking to be superior as a means to counteract this feeling of inferiority. This is why many feel the need to outdo others, or to work themselves silly, just so they can appear to be the kingpin amongst their friends and family. When we turn our backs upon our true nature as Spirit, then we turn our backs upon the abundant nature of the inner God. We cannot encounter the nature of this inner abundance, until we wake up to that God within. When we turn our backs on Spirit, what comes into play is this dishevelled substitute called ego. This mentality seeks outside of itself, amongst the dust, the scraps and the toys of the world, to find some resemblance of sustenance, to keep its ineffective and disheartening emptiness at bay.

When the ego has us in despair, we may find ourselves trying to fill the cavities we feel within with items of a material nature. This is now the modern way of relieving our feelings of emptiness. Retail therapy is what it has become known as. The next new toy is going to make everything all right for 'me', and then I'll maybe allow myself to be happy. Of course, if we can temporarily alleviate our sense of inferiority, by convincing ourselves that someone else is jealous of our new toys, then we have killed two birds with the one stone, haven't we? Not only do we gain a sense of temporary happiness, we also get to feel superior. Well, we do for just a little while anyway until the buzz of getting the new toy wears off, and we then notice once again this lack of meaning, this deadness and unfulfilling void within.

We have indeed, to differing degrees developed a sense of worthlessness within ourselves, due to the ego which we dance to the tune of. We then think that the only way to counteract this sense of worthlessness is to define our worth by the collection of material possessions, status and wealth that we have acquired. Even our children are plagued with this mode of mind. It is reported in the United Kingdom, that the main cause of bullying in schools, is due to a child not wearing trainers that carry a recognizable brand name. So, if a child comes to school wearing trainers which have not been made by one of the big names, then that child will most certainly be bullied.

When we are saturated with this egoic mentality, we may also use job titles to give ourselves the illusion of better-ness. We mistakenly use these job titles, in a manner as if they are part and parcel of what we are. Not only do we have our name as an identity, but we also identify with our job as being 'me' also. For example, take the following scenario.

"Hi there. I'm Bill and I'm a Doctor"

"Wooo" we say to ourselves, *"Now I'm going to rub shoulders with this guy, he's important, and if I'm friends with him I'll also be seen as being important."*

Now, along comes our old friend John, and we know that John has a job as a bin man. But we don't want to be seen with bin men, what would people think of us? Hell, they may even think that we are bin men also, and then we would be taking a major drop in our illusory social status. We couldn't have that, as we may then feel inferior and we don't want to feel inferior, because we spend every ounce of our energy trying to escape from our egos persistent feelings of inferiority. We are here with our new friend the doctor, this makes us feel superior, to be socializing with a high class social giant as our friend the doctor. So, I guess our old buddy John can go and get stuffed can't he?

We seek for this kind of status and for some great standing within a divisive society, which is run by that egoic mind system that we have called the rat race. The rat race is of course the egos never-ending need to outdo others at all costs. It is our tendency to work ourselves silly so we can become what has been termed a 'success' within the egos system. All of this however is a dismal attempt at offsetting this lack and emptiness we feel within ourselves. It also reinforces that feeling of separation we feel from life and Spirit.

If we are caught in this rat race mentality, then we most likely have stress as our closest chum. We think of ourselves as being this great idea of 'success', but we don't even allow ourselves to enjoy whatever level of success we have obtained, due to this stressful rat race mind-set. We cannot genuinely enjoy any real success in life, if we have sought it only in an attempt to alleviate the pain of the egos inferiority. Any buzz we get from this rat race version of success, is like a drug which we get a temporary high from, only to come back down again with the low hangover of realism. Yes, realism will surely come knocking upon each of our doors sooner or later, and sadly when we are caught deeply within the egos world, we find it all the harder to hear that knocking on the door.

At this moment I am reminded of a saying I once heard. This saying sums up the rat race mentality perfectly. Let me share it with you, it goes something like this - *"The trouble with the rat race is - even if you 'win', at the end of it all, you're still a rat."*

A rat - is that what we really want to be? If however, we awakened to what is going on within our awareness, then as a result of that awakening we could see clearly the uselessness of the meagre offerings, which the ego tries to hold our attention with. Then perhaps, we would realize that the egos offerings are irrelevant indeed, and as a result of that realization we may actually drop the ego from our awareness totally. This limited and robotic egoic system, of how things work here upon our Earth leaves no room for improvement at all. Most of us are heavily engrossed in this egoic system, which is clearly failing. We are now totally out of accord with nature and indeed our own true nature within. Yes dreamland is where most of us reside, and we are completely oblivious to the fact that we are sleeping in daydreams of make believe.

None of us seem to be truly fulfilled by this egoic system, but we bury our heads in the sand just like the Ostrich, and then pretend that all is going well for us. Yet at this moment of our time, there is very little that any of us can actually do physically about this egoic world system. We all follow this system blindly because our minds are completely sleeping in dreamland. Therefore we are unable to use our minds collectively, in order to agree upon some other way. Perhaps we will only ever find another way, when we finally shake off our collective insanity. Insanity is the cause of all the world's problems, and *sanity* is the only solution to these problems, because insanity can only ever create more insanity.

Now, at this moment in our time, we are childishly insane, and that's a simple fact. We are so insane in fact, that I have always figured that if aliens were really visiting this planet, then I know exactly why they don't land a space ship out in the open and say *"Hi Guys"*. They most likely think of us all as being like the living dead. We probably frighten them. Actually I'm very surprised by the number of reported UFO sightings, still being reported from around the world. These aliens must not have any sense at all, or they would have turned their space ships around long ago, and hot tailed it right back to wherever they came from. I'm surprised that they are not worried we might one day capture them, and then use their spaceships to head for their own home planet - so we can 'civilize' them, or worse still - so we can 'save' them.

Now, the natural peace of the inner God, which we were all born with, will not be realized within us as long as we subscribe to the egoic world system (the rat race). This system of operating drives the hypnotic spell of thought further into our awareness. We substitute our abundant spiritual nature, for a shabby materialistic replacement. This need not be the case however, just because the whole world is saturated in it, doesn't mean that we have to be saturated in it also. We can leave this view of the world behind forever, by choosing the Spirit instead. Then we live our lives from the Spirit and not f om the ego. We

178

will no longer be fooled into thinking that our fulfilment resides in material acquirements, job titles and so called social 'status'.

Instead of seeing the world as the hell that the ego would have us see it as, we see the world as it really is. We would then see the world in its natural state, whenever we are aware of our natural state. How do we experience the world then, when we shift our attention to the God within? We then experience our planet as no less than the Kingdom of Heaven!

Eliminating the trash:

When we find ourselves interested in spiritual awakening, it's usually because we are looking for solace and relief from the pain we have generated within our mind, due to our dabbling in the egos world. We may, if we are lucky, come upon a teacher who will tell us quite directly that the source of many of our problems is our very own gloomy thinking. Then he may offer a simple remedy to eliminate this gloomy thinking. Perhaps our teacher will let us know that the Spirit is very much alive within us all. Only these dark thoughts which we fill our awareness with, will ever block out this natural peace from our awareness. A helpful teacher may inform us that the pain which we feel within is a knock on effect coming from the dark thoughts we hold in our mind. We think and then we experience the effects of our thoughts, with our emotions. This is where emotional stress makes its debut, upon the stage of our lives.

But do we actually look into our own thought processes? Do we actually consider that the darkness which we need to loosen from our lives, resides within our own mind? We think that eliminating the thought trash from our lives involves altering our outer behaviour and manner of speech. Yet our outer behaviour and speech is nothing more than the knock-on effect of the thoughts we hold within our own mind. The mouth will always speak what the mind is full of, and the body will always act according to the instructions the mind (thought) gives it.

We may also feel that eliminating what we call 'negativity' has to do with getting rid of 'negative' people from our lives. But, don't you know that like attracts like. So we will always find ourselves being most friendly with those who share our interests and passions, and with those who share our thoughts. As soon as we change our interests; let's say for example that we don't want to have dark thought dramas in our mind anymore, and we decide to drop darkness from our awareness altogether, then we will most definitely find a change occurring in our friendships. Why is this? Well, because those people who we once discussed our mad dramas with, won't like the fact that we are not there anymore for the old familiar styled conversations, and all of that annoying hurly burly mental drama stuff. Now, do you think these friends will be supportive of you, when you want to clear your mind of dark thought dramas? I don't think so, seriously, do you?

However, we must be sure not to walk the road of the judgemental hypocrite when this change in friendship occurs. We should be focused on clearing our own mind of trash. What other people hold in their mind is absolutely none of our business. However, what we hold in our mind is also none of our friends business either. Sadly though, the eventual outcome of these friendships just mentioned will be a withering away effect – that is, if you do indeed stick to your guns, keeping your mind clear of upsetting and downbeat trash thought dramas.

Usually we let all that trash build up, until it snowballs into a great avalanche within our mind and it weighs down heavily upon our nervous system, until we are at breaking point. We get smothered by it, as it overflows into our lives, turning our everyday existence into a nightmarish version of hell. Then we gradually and maybe reluctantly, view all of the thoughts swirling in our mind as useless absurdity. When we have reached this point, our muscles can no longer bear the claustrophobic weight of thought and our world becomes dark;

we want to break free of this thought created existence, as life has now become empty of any true meaning, and then all of a sudden - *Kablooey!*

Out we throw all of the trash dramas we have been cherishing. Out goes the effort of 'becoming' a spiritual stereotype. It all falls away from us and we are not even bothered with cleaning up the fallout. We surrender, waving the white flag, exclaiming to the universe, *"I'm finished, I'm done, I'm not playing your game anymore. Do your worst because I don't care anymore!"*

Now does the little 'me' (ego) give up its throne just like that? Does it suddenly cease its strategic game of make believe, when we have reached this stage? Sadly not completely, however, we now know its every move and every trick. We are now no longer interested in, or fascinated by its web of illusion. We have finally reached a point in our mental evolution, when we prefer Reality over the egos dreamland. We have our eye squarely on the target - Reality! The ego, will no longer completely cast its mesmerizing spell over us ever again. For a short while, we will notice the habitual momentum of the old thoughts, still churning and spinning within our awareness; but that habitual thought momentum slows down each time we step out of it. It is then no longer being propelled by our attention, interest and fascination. We realize that only our interest in the egos world, was what kept it spinning within our awareness. Now, if that interest is totally gone, then the momentum of thought will naturally slow down until it reaches a final cessation.

And then - All is placid. The grand game of life has had its relentless turbulence eased and we find that the One/God was always there within us, although dormant and unexpressed due to the mind made 'me' (ego) dancing in our awareness, seeking for our attention with its never ending dramas. Now that we know this, we don't stir up our minds anymore and we sure as hell won't let anybody else stir our minds up either.

Now, do we have to come to a dark place in our experience of life, before we finally let that phantom of ego go from our mind? Maybe not, maybe we are a very adventurous person who is thrilled and excited about the prospects of spiritual awakening. As an adventurer, possibly we will boldly jump into that awareness like a scientist in search of the absolute truth. I don't totally feel that the dark night of the soul scenario, is a necessity or a prerequisite for everybody. Most sincere Truth seekers will all come to a point when they will need to find the Reality which they have been searching so ardently for. We cannot keep our search for Spirit simply as an entertainment forever. The Spirit will not tolerate our delay tactics and will most assuredly knock heavy and hard upon the door of our lives, until we pay attention and wake up!

When we do pay attention and wake up to Reality, there we will find the peace of the God within, that seemed to be evading us all along. However when we awaken to this Spirit of God within, we will realize that it was not the peace of God that had been evading us all of this time ... *It is we who have been evading the peace of God!*

16

Dialogues 2

Q: You say that too much philosophy can confuse us, but don't we have to read books before we can find a way that works?

A: Yes, we do have to read some books or maybe listen to one or two teachers, because we need someone to point the way, but where does it all end? What happens after you read the book or listen to the teacher? Do you awaken, or do you even use what you have read in those books at all? More often than not, most seekers usually read tons of books, and never ever get around to the waking up part. They usually settle for philosophy or beliefs instead.

I read tons of spiritual books during the years of my search, and at the end of it all I didn't know whether I was coming or going. One book would say to do nothing, yet another book would tell you to meditate 2 or 3 times a day. Other books would suggest delving into the dark recesses of your unconscious, and others would have you trying to locate a hypnotist who could regress you into your past life to heal the illusive 'pain' there too. It can all get quite ridiculous really.

At the end of my search, I finally narrowed my focus down to a few books I had, which simplified the teachings of how thought and belief can contaminate our reality; they also simplified the teachings of presence for me. I finally used what those few simple books suggested. But at that point in my search I was finally _ready_ to use what I had read. I was no longer satisfied with just thinking or talking about it all. I wanted freedom from the tormenting voice in my head. Now, that's all that is required before you will ever allow awakening to occur - you have to want awakening more than you want the voice in your head!

A complete beginner could awaken, immediately upon hearing their first clear teaching on awakening. It all depends upon how much you are willing to allow that shift in your attention from thought to Reality. In fact, I knew a man once who read *one* book, and no more than one, and it resulted in his awakening. He was ready to let go and move beyond thought, that's all. So, it took no time for him, just the simple understanding that his own thinking was the problem, and that presence was the cure. When he realized this, he fully desired awakening more than his thought dramas. Thus, awakening was the result.

Q: That would be a rare case you're talking about though, wouldn't it be?

A: Maybe it is a rare case, simply because many who claim to want awakening, are more interested in reading and seeking rather than simple *finding*. They read supposed 'channelled' books or seeming 'non-dual' books; they run to this guru or that spiritual workshop, or we have them trying to figure out how the universe came into existence. All and any of this will do, simply because it keeps the seeking game alive.

Q: But what's wrong with that?

A: Nothing's wrong with that, as long as you don't end up hypnotized by it all. Trust me, if you really are interested in pure awakening, then you won't want to saturate your mind with a whole lot of old words and talk. You'll end up believing everything, but realizing *nothing!* That's how you become hypnotized. It's easy to spot one who is hypnotized by second hand philosophy and beliefs. All you have to do is say something different from what they believe, and if they are hypnotized, they will react strongly or maybe even viciously. These types of seekers haven't reached that tipping point yet, simply because they aren't willing to be simpleminded. Now, by simpleminded, I don't mean dumb or stupid, only simple within your mind-set.

Some folks want to philosophize, debate and seek forever, and that's okay, it *really* is, I always say, because it is just as valid a hobby as any other, but here we are talking about awakening, not hobbies. If those in search of awakening could only keep everything simple, and keep their mind free from complexity and all the intellectual head stuff, then they would awaken with great ease. So far, I've found that those who *do* awaken, are simply those who have reached a point where they have had their absolute fill of thought dramas – even the thought dramas of spiritual entertainment.

Q: But we still have to read until we find the technique that works, don't we?

A: I don't know if you are ready to hear the simple truth yet or not, but you have to realize that the only way which really works for _everybody_ at the end of the day, is just simple presence. Presence is the best way to meditate; really it's the only effective way to meditate, since you should be taking that presence into everything that you do. It's a 24-7 thing, you know? Now, this isn't only *my* teaching here; any decent teacher worth their salt will be saying the *exact* same thing. All meditation and spiritual practice is meant to facilitate the awakening of spiritual awareness as a 24-7 thing. Now, remaining present throughout each day is the only way to facilitate this 24-7 awakening of spiritual awareness. Reading philosophy won't do it, that's for sure. All philosophy will do is fill your mind with thought, and will convince you that you already know all about the true nature of your Reality, when you actually won't, you'll just _believe_ that you do.

If you made it a habit to live every moment of every day in absolute presence, then you'll really come to know your true spiritual nature. If you are relaxing or taking a nap, then relax or nap in presence, and if you are going for a walk or working hard, then walk and work hard in presence. It's a habit one develops quite quickly whenever it becomes the main _priority_ in your life. Making it the priority of your life is the best thing you can do for you and your life. You'll then see everything afresh, and relate to everything in life in a new and liberating way.

Q: Sometimes I have to deal with very aggressive people; they get me down and I end up stressed in their company. I find that an uplifting spiritual book will steady me, and get me back on track.

_A:_ Yes, some good books can certainly do that alright, but we can't keep relying upon books forever, now can we? There comes a day when we will have meet the world head on. The books only point to Reality or awakening, but it's up to us to use what these books say, otherwise they are a waste of paper, not to mention money. Whenever the road seems rocky, or whenever you are overwhelmed after dealing with an aggressive person, well then, by all means dip into an inspiring book, but remember to use what you read, or else what is the point in reading it at all?

Q: How do you usually deal with aggressive people?

_A:_ I try not to deal with them anymore. I find them to be boring individuals.

Q: But we all have these people in our lives.

A: Yes we do, and I suppose we do have to deal with them sometimes, but I mainly ignore them as best I can. It's either that or I get away from them. These days I view aggressive people much in the same way as I would view an upsetting thought. I treat these people in the same way as I would treat that thought - I just ignore them.

Q: But sometimes they are really in my face, and it's hard to ignore them.

A: I know what you mean; sometimes listening to these types is a bit like hearing nails being scraped along a blackboard. We have to deal with these people as best we see fit. I no longer want to deal with them at all. There are far too many nice people in this world, for me to be bothered with aggressive people. I prefer to keep madness completely out of my mind. Since I no longer tolerate madness in my own mind, I am certainly not going to let others implant madness into my mind.

However, I always say that nobody is a Superman. At times, I too find that listening to the monotonous blabber of these aggressive types can occasionally drain me a little. These types would drain anybody, if you were exposed too much to them. They can act much like vampires, sucking on your spiritual energy. So that's why I would suggest either ignoring them, or preferably getting away from them altogether.

Generally, if you keep your mind free of thought dramas these types shouldn't get you down too much. It's really only if you carry what they say into your own mind, and then start thinking about it, that you end up getting upset. So try to remain present at all times, keep your own mind free of thought dramas, and you'll find that the madness of others won't get you down so much.

Q: There are so many thoughts coming and going all of the time; how can we possibly clear them all away? It sounds like something only a super person could do.

A: I have some news for you; as long as you believe that awakening is a super human thing, then that very belief will stand in the way of your awakening. That's why I suggest that you should examine some of your beliefs surrounding awakening. Those kind of beliefs will keep you chasing after awakening forever.

Q: How can we keep our mind clear in every moment of life? That would be like practicing a technique indefinitely.

A: You don't need to practice anything to become aware of truth. If it's true then it doesn't need cultivating, just realized. You realize it when you leave your awareness clear of thought; then maybe there can be some room left in your awareness for the Spirit to be realized. You don't have to go around fighting with your thoughts you know; just ignore them, whether they are good or bad, and cast your attention out through your senses upon life instead.

This doesn't take practice, just a simple willingness or desire to let go of the mind clutter. Why would you want to hold onto that mind clutter anyway? Is it for entertainment purposes perhaps? You know if people had a few more hobbies to get them out of the house, then they would have no need to be creating mental movies inside their heads to entertain themselves all the time. Could it be that we think we will become bored if we switched off the mental movies? Don't you see that thought is the cause of boredom? It is the sole source of all annoyance, stress and despondency in life. But some people are attached to all of that annoying stuff, they haven't had their fill of it yet, so on goes the dream until they do have their fill of it, if they ever do!

Once the scales tip over from the desire to stay asleep to the desire for awakening, then keeping your mind clear becomes irrelevant, because you'll find that when the desire for awakening burns fiercely within you, you will automatically begin paying attention to the now quite effortlessly. When thought is ignored and disinterest sets in with regard to the content of thought, then the momentum of thought begins to wither. It slows down all on its own, due to your lack of interest in it.

Q: But setting aside some quiet time to practice presence can still help to prepare for awakening, can it not?

A: The *Real* isn't something which is lurking outside of the everyday mundane life you know. You don't have to set aside time for this. With every task you do, the *Real* is always present there – you just aren't paying attention fully to what you are doing, that's all. Your attention is divided between the doing and what you are thinking about. Maybe you are shopping for groceries and instead of actually being there, fully attentive to the shop you are in (the sounds of the shop, the smells of the shop etc), you maybe have your attention locked up in some fantasy land of thought instead. Hence, the present Reality eludes you.

So pay full attention to the now of your doing (whatever it is) and there you will find the *Real.* It doesn't take practice; it just takes the desire to get real. What do you choose; thought or Reality? Which seems more enticing, staying asleep in your dreams of thought or awakening with absolute ease to the present Reality of the One, as it is, here and now? This isn't going to magically happen all on its own you know, despite what some teachers and gurus say.

You have to ask yourself the important question - do you really want this? If you find your thought content entertaining, then you won't allow your attention to shift out of that thought content, it's as simple as that. There is no harm in the thought content, just as long as it leans more towards happy dreams rather than depressing thought-mares. So, are you happy with your thought content? Do you find it entertaining to be day dreaming all day long? If you do, then you can forget about awakening, because you won't find enough desire to fuel the awakening of spiritual awareness. Without a desire for Truth, the flame won't be kept burning.

Q: Can a spiritual practice not help to grow awareness of Oneness within us?

A: When awareness awakens out of the daydreams, then we become aware of what has always been within us and all around us. Spiritual practices can at best bring us some temporary spiritual experiences, which are nice to have, but true and lasting awakening only comes about as a result of our burning desire to be free in Reality. No practice can make us desire Reality over thought. We either desire it or we don't. The desire starts to burn in us when we reach a point when we are ready to trust in the unknown to guide us. Are we ready to give up the control, the manipulation and the demands we make upon life?

Q: It's all well and good sitting around talking about spirituality; anyone can talk about it, but it's a person's actions that really count, not their words.

A: Actually, *true* spirituality does not depend upon actions or words. That's just more control and manipulation you are talking about, which the ego uses to keep us chasing after freedom forever. Awakening is only about pure realization in one's own experience and that alone. This realization is not a thought generated act. In fact, putting on the 'holy' act, only ever serves to interfere with this realization. The 'holy' performance is what the world has been faced with for long enough now. The religions have kept this pretence up for millennia, and now the new age movement is falling into the same old trap.

The childish pictures we have in our minds of awakened guys being super 'good' guys who walk slowly, talk softly, hug trees, smile all the time, and pretend to like everybody in the world, is absolute nonsense. This 'holy' act has gotten old and tired; it's played out and downright hypocritical. If you're really interested in awakening to Reality, then you should leave the 'holy' act to the religions, egoic gurus and the spiritual entertainment seekers of the world. If you really want awakening, then you should join the ranks of the true and _authentic_ Reality guys out there.

The 'holy' act, of trying to behave in the manner in which we think an awakened person should behave, is just ridiculous. When we pretend to be very 'spiritual' we cannot avoid being hypocritical. Since we are involved in judging our own behaviour, we cannot avoid judging the behaviour of others as being 'unspiritual'. We usually begin this act by trying to become a spiritual stereotype person, because we mistakenly believe that becoming this stereotype will make us ready receptacles for spiritual realization. But we already have that Spirit within us, so we are therefore _now_ receptacles holding Gods Spirit within us. Altering our behaviour, speech or lifestyle to imitate what we think spiritual looks like is a fool's game. Awakening has damn all to do with your behaviour, your words or your choice of lifestyle, but has everything to do with how clear your awareness is, or how cluttered with thought it is.

After awakening you will find that certain aspects of your mannerisms or lifestyle will change, but they will change _naturally_, it's not forced or pretended. Pretence will never make way for awakening; it will only get in the way because you are trying to alter yourself with thought in order to construct a new thought made spiritual identity, a new spiritual 'me' - a new 'spiritual' looking ego. Now that's a really boring old game to be playing, I know, trust me, I've been down that silly old joyless road. Stop acting spiritual and realize that you are _already_ spiritual. Stop pretending, stop imitating and stop trying to become, become, become. Dare to let yourself be _real_ - let your awareness clear for a while, and just see what happens then.

Consider this; if there was nobody in the world to watch you perform your 'spiritual' act, would you bother with it at all?

Once your mind clears of trash thought, then the behaviour which once emanated from that thought also disappears, so you won't end up as a 'bad' guy by letting go of this silly behaviour control. Are you putting on a spiritual act so others will think good thoughts about you? Is it important for you to be seen as being the stereotype spiritual person? If the answer to these two questions is *yes*, then you are lost in the egos game of becoming, and you are interfering with your true natural expression. You are interfering with the Spirits flowing nature. I've noticed that spiritual actors rarely ever let that game go.

Q: I always thought spirituality meant changing yourself for the better. How can we awaken without changing our ways?

A: We don't have to change; awakening automatically brings the change with it. All we have to 'do' is allow the awareness to clear of thoughts. Anything which seems like 'bad' behaviour, only ever arises from our thoughts. When those thoughts are gone, then the behaviour takes care of itself. Then you'll see what really is, rather than what you think *should* be. You'll then be at peace within yourself, and as a result you'll also be at peace with everyone else.

Q: Do you think that's the answer to world peace?

A: That's a big question. Many factors would have to come into play to bring about something as big as world peace. Theoretically, if everyone on the planet allowed peace within themselves, then yes, world peace could happen very quickly. However, many are not interested in being peaceful at all. There are far too many trouble makers around. There are around 6.5 billion of us in this world, so I can't see everyone allowing peace. They all want 'peace' on their own terms and that can't happen. Minds clash with opposing minds; though only when we go beyond mind does peace really arise.

Our species is predominantly insane; not everyone is insane, but unfortunately some of the guys in power are completely mad, and they want to keep war and mayhem ongoing whilst they show a smile to the cameras. They hypnotize the populace through the media with propaganda and lies, and then once they have everyone believing their stories, they can do whatever they want. You have to want peace for it to ever happen, but due to collective insanity, I can't see world peace happening in my lifetime, but let's hope I'm wrong.

Q: What do you think causes collective insanity?

A: Another big question. Many things cause it and all I can do is theorize about what causes it. I suppose fear and greed seem to be the main reasons for insanity, but religious beliefs also cause people to get crazy. Many identify with a particular religion, they make it part of their sense of 'me', which then causes division into 'me' against 'you' or 'us' against 'them'. Many would also like to maintain insanity, simply for the drama it brings to their lives.

However, all insanity is still caused by *thought*. The cure for insanity is to move beyond thought. However, you can't force sanity on people; if they don't want it, then they won't have it. Some don't even believe they are good enough for sanity or awakening. They think it's too hard to achieve, or that it will cost too much of their time and attention. They think they have to 'do' a lot, or practice a lot before they can be at peace or awaken to the present Oneness of Reality.

Q: I feel awake most of the time, and I am nearly always aware of 'what is', but it still feels like maybe there is something else which I have to 'do'.

A: That doesn't make any sense to me. If you feel awake and are always aware of 'what is', then you certainly wouldn't feel like there was something else to do. You would realize that this is very natural whenever it is your priority in life. Remaining awake depends upon whether or not it is a priority, simply because staying in the here and now happens moment to moment, it's a 24-7 thing. It's a preference for Reality over cloud cuckoo land. If you have lots of other little 'priorities' more important than that, then you will allow your mind to become cluttered with all of those little scraps of thought.

By the way, the best thing you can do for others and your own life in general is to become clear and present in the now; first and foremost. You'll be a nicer person for others to be around, and your life will feel like it is running more smoothly. That's why it's better to put the horse before the cart with regard to your priorities. Some people feel like they are being selfish if they put their own sanity above everything else in life, but really it's the best thing you can do for everyone and everything in your life. Insane or unstable people are usually not very nice people to be around, and they usually screw everything up also. Now, you are either awake or you are not, you say you feel awake most of the time, well which is it?

Q: Well, at times I feel energy moving in my body. There are different spiritual experiences I have had, although they don't last very long. That's why I wonder if there is something else I need to do.

A: Many people feel like they are awake just because they have had some momentary spiritual experiences. But I've noticed that seekers tend to chase after spiritual experiences in the same way that a junkie chases after their fix of drugs. This leaves you like a prisoner; a slave to the addiction of spiritual experiences. Are you a spiritual addict looking for your fix? I think you are confusing an experience with being awake. Awakening does indeed bring what could be called a new flavour of 'experience' into one's life; a fresher, cleaner, unifying, crystal clear clarity of perception, but it isn't like an experience which comes and goes. This clarity remains as long as we don't slip back into dreamland. Because of that clarity of mind, energetic spiritual experiences will certainly come and go more frequently, but because of their impermanent nature, one should not really get all that hung up on them.

If you were really awake, then you would no longer be looking for anything else to 'do'. You only think there is more to 'do', because we have been conditioned to believe that awakening is about achieving some fixed and static blissfully energetic state. Nobody and I repeat _nobody_ remains in a fixed state of bliss mixed with ecstatic energetic experiences all the time, and anyone who says that they do is a liar!

We think awakening has to do with kundalini experiences, or seeing auras and celestial beings, being psychic and mind reading. Awakening has absolutely nothing to do with these temporary experiences. Awakening really has to do with simply staying free of the thought spell and living in _Reality_. I've met many people who have had pretty powerful and energetic spiritual experiences, and they still remain as total slaves to thought. This is simply because, after the experience wore off, they still found the thought spell to be so damn alluring. I think many spiritual teachers fall into that category. In fact, recently I heard about a spiritual teacher who was living in New York, he had no bother igniting energetic spiritual experiences in his students, but then he ended up killing himself one day, much to the shock and dismay of his loyal followers. So, the temporary experiences are not what we need to be seeking for.

Really, awakening is the easiest thing in the whole wide world, and Attentive Presence couldn't be easier. However, we do need to _honestly_ decide if it's what we really want, because if it isn't, then we won't stick with presence. Now, there is absolutely nothing we have to '_do_' to wake up. Paying attention to the moment is not something which needs to be 'done'. It's a mode of living and operating; it's a mode of being. Filling your mind up with a whole lot of old nonsensical thought scenarios takes a hell of a lot of 'doing'. With awakening you actually _cease_ your constant and never ending mental 'doing', as you allow your attention to shift casually and effortlessly into the present.

Q: *I don't think it's as easy as that.*

A: Well then – As you think, so shall it be! When someone says to me, *"it's not as easy as that"*, then I know that I'm talking to someone who has either become confused through listening to far too many spiritual sideshow teachers, or to someone who is just looking for an excuse to remain asleep in dreamland. You don't need an excuse to remain in dreamland, you know? It's your awareness and it's nobody else's business what you allow your awareness to be filled with. If you are enjoying your dreamland, then that's okay, but if you are really interested in awakening, then quit with the excuses and allow realization to occur in your awareness once and for all.

If it is lack of understanding you suffer from, then ask yourself this question - Is paying attention to life as it is happening right now, really all that difficult? Is it difficult to pay attention? It takes more effort to live in dreamland. It takes no effort at all to stop and live in peace. Peace and effort cannot go together; it doesn't even make sense to say that it takes effort to find peace of mind. Effort is equal to stress. The cessation of effort is equal to perfect equanimity and peace. Is it really that difficult to simply stop and live in the here and now – to drink through your senses all that life brings, moment to moment?

Q: *Didn't you have to spend over ten years searching before you finally awakened?*

A: I spent over ten years wasting my time, because I was so fascinated with the whole spiritual sideshow malarkey. I spent ten years burdening my mind with second hand philosophies, beliefs and spiritual rules of becoming. I listened to far too many spiritual sideshow teachers. I chased after the temporary spiritual highs. I was a stereotype new ager. But all of that stuff only ever served to get in my way, even though seekers like to think that it all helps. That mish mash of new age and spiritual philosophy leaves the mind confused, thinking that it already knows what awakening is, when it actually doesn't.

It wasn't until I got fed up with the thought dramas, that I finally let them go and switched into Reality. That didn't take any time; it just took a _willingness_ to get real once and for all. I then threw out all of the philosophies, the beliefs, the sideshow gurus and every other thing I burdened my mind with. In short; I threw out all thought dramas. I asked myself that question; Is it really that difficult to simply stop with the effort, and live in the here and now? I found that living for the moment wasn't difficult at all, it only appeared to be, because I was too busy philosophizing about it all. So you should stop your philosophizing, stop your gathering of second hand beliefs; stop thinking and start living, it's as easy as that!

Q: With a very busy routine in life, sometimes I wonder if I stopped, would the world stop too.

_A:_ Yes, been there, got the t-shirt. You equate physical action with mental doing. You don't have to stop physically, in order to keep your attention in the here and now. We all have this silly picture in our mind, of the spiritual guy sitting cross legged on top of a mountain in total solitude, and we think, that's what it will take for me to allow the mental traffic to quieten down. That's all nonsense of course.

However, it does take a little _trust_ to let go of the mind stuff, to hand the reigns over to the Spirit, or life flow instead. Trust me, when you mentally give up and begin to live life in the moment, you'll get more done, and the quality of what you do will be much better. You'll also be able to go at it like a work horse, with more energy, better efficiency and still have energy to spare when you're done with whatever it is that you are doing. You just got to understand that mental noise interferes with your life and everything that you do. It poisons everything, from relationships, to things you want to achieve; it makes enemies out of innocent people and ruins your level of happiness also. If you can only trust that the Spirit can do things much better than a mind which is filled up with trash thought, then letting go into the now moment should be effortless for you.

Q: Maybe we just need to say "to hell with it" in a very loud voice, and then we will awaken.

A: I like your style. Yes, just say *"to hell with it"*, to the whole lot of it; all of the silly stuff which keeps your mind spinning out of control. What else is there to say to that kind of trash? I guess you could call that the modern vernacular for surrender. However, most people don't like letting go in this way. They like getting themselves all dirty from rolling around in the mental trash heap. It makes their lives seem a little less boring, like something is happening all the time. Inside their mind they have their own private soap opera running 24-7; their little story titled *'The Adventures of Me'*. I suppose it's only when we have had enough of rolling around in the trash heap that we will allow ourselves to surrender, and then say *"to hell with it"*.

Q: I've heard it said that awakened people usually abandon normal life, like family, friends etc, after awakening occurs. They usually live a more reclusive kind of life – is that true?

A: After awakening you will go with the flow of life, and where the flow don't go, you don't go. So whatever happens is whatever happens, you are done manipulating life or trying to control it. There's no more rules, no more stereotypical behaviour. You are life, simply flowing along at your ease. Sometimes you may find that things will change, but they may remain the same. You may change your job or not. You may move house or not. You may find yourself socializing with different people or not.

There is no fixed stereotypical scenario which will play itself out. Life goes on and things happen, just as normal. My outer life hasn't changed a lot. I'm more active now, whereas beforehand I was somewhat lazy. I found that strange, since I once upon a time thought that awakened folks sat around all day in a meditative posture doing damn all. I used to think that awakened people packed their job in, and lived saintly lives up in the hills.

Q: From all that you are saying, it seems that what we have been searching for has always been the case, and we just weren't looking in the right place.

A: Yes, very well put, that's about the height of it. We have had our noses stuck in books galore; as if our true nature could ever be found inside a book. We have been trying to figure out Reality with thought, through our philosophies, our religions and our beliefs. We have been searching for gurus and all manner of wise guys to bow down to. We have been waiting upon a temporary ecstatic experience of transcendental bliss and euphoria etc. Yet no temporary experience will ever have a lasting effect; it always fades leaving us wondering, where did it all go wrong? We have been trying to imitate the awakened, by acting out the stereotypes of how we think the awakened should behave. We have been amusing ourselves with constant seeking, and more importantly, we have been amusing ourselves with constant thought dramas.

But it's all just thought dramas at the end of the day; all of this distraction I've mentioned. We have allowed ourselves to fall prey to the hypnotic melody of religion or the gurus' words, words, words and endless words. And all the while, the *Real* no-thing that we are has been here all along, just waiting for us to recognize it once again.

So yes, we haven't been looking in the right place, we have been looking everywhere else *apart* from the right place. Yet the present moment, where Reality is to be found, is always here, right under our noses. The Spirit has always been within us, trying to illuminate our awareness with its essence, but we have lots of other stuff taking up space in our awareness, don't we? With all of the thought dramas we hold onto, what room will there ever be in our awareness, to know anything else but those thought dramas?

So, most Truth seekers are certainly seeking for something, but with most, that something is certainly not Reality. However, Reality is always the case; and even logically, it can only ever be discovered in the here and now, that present moment which all true spiritual teachers talk about. There's nothing to 'become' in order to be aware of Truth. There's no purification needed to be in alignment with your natural self. No effort, no discipline, no practice. That Truth is with you even as you hear these words. It's there within you and all around you, whether you believe me or disbelieve me. It will emerge into your awareness when you leave some space for it. So go ahead now, divert your attention out of thought and see this moment as it is - listen to this moment as it is - feel this moment as it is - smell and taste this moment as it is, and now, behold the Oneness of Reality!

The awakening of spiritual awareness arises as you pay attention to the here and now. It arises as you divert your attention to simple everyday life as it is happening all around you. The One is always there, with every move you make and with every breath you take - and that's just how the song goes.

CPSIA information can be obtained at www.ICGtesting.com
Printed in the USA
LVOW13s1609270514

387445LV00002B/461/P